Why Global Justice Matters

For Sophia, Felix, Leonard and Yasmin

Why Global Justice Matters

Moral Progress in a Divided World

Chris Armstrong

polity

First published in 2019 by Polity Press

Polity Press
65 Bridge Street
Cambridge CB2 1UR, UK

Polity Press
101 Station Landing
Suite 300
Medford, MA 02155, USA

ISBN-13: 978-1-5095-3187-5
ISBN-13: 978-1-5095-3188-2(pb)

A catalogue record for this book is available from the British Library.

Library of Congress Cataloging-in-Publication Data
Names: Armstrong, C. (Chris), 1965- author.
Title: Why global justice matters : moral progress in a divided world / Chris
    Armstrong.
Description: Cambridge, UK ; Medford, MA, USA : Polity Press, [2019] |
    Includes bibliographical references and index.
Identifiers: LCCN 2018049134 (print) | LCCN 2018061137 (ebook) | ISBN
    9781509536214 (Epub) | ISBN 9781509531875 | ISBN 9781509531882 (pb)
Subjects: LCSH: Social justice. | Social justice--International cooperation.
    | Globalization--Moral and ethical aspects. | Western
    countries--Relations--Developing countries. | Developing
    countries--Relations--Western countries.
Classification: LCC HM671 (ebook) | LCC HM671 .A76 2019 (print) | DDC
    303.3/72--dc23
LC record available at https://lccn.loc.gov/2018049134

Typeset in 11 on 14 pt Sabon by Servis Filmsetting Ltd, Stockport, Cheshire
Printed and bound in Great Britain by CPI Group (UK) Ltd, Croydon

Contents

Preface

Our world is, on the whole, a much more prosperous and peaceful place than the one our grandparents and their grandparents knew. Recent decades have brought enormous changes to human life expectancy, partly because of new treatments for diseases that would have snuffed out countless lives in the past. For the average inhabitant of our planet, sanitary conditions and access to healthcare have improved dramatically. Meanwhile universal education, mass public transport and the internet have opened up new worlds. Mass warfare, though never far from the news, appears to be declining. The second half of the twentieth century also brought a great wave of democratization which, though a decidedly unfinished revolution, put political power in the hands of millions of the people for the first time. For the average person, it seems, things are simply getting better and better.

But the world is not populated by statistics and averages. It is home to individual people whose lives often bear little trace of the apparently smooth progress captured in the last paragraph. Despite the immense progress made in our world as a whole, the planet we all inhabit is characterized by enormous inequality. Whilst many of us have grown used to affluence, others continue to make do with very little. Hundreds of millions of people live in conditions of terrible poverty, and in many parts of the world things are scarcely improving at all. Though the global economy continues to grow, for the most part it brings ever-greater benefits to those who are already doing well. The winners continue to win, and the losers still lose. Half a century and more has passed since the great wave of decolonization swept our world. But in many cases those who have prospered since have been the citizens of the former colonial powers, rather than the countries which they ruled over. Though many of us hope for change, international organizations all too often represent the interests of the wealthy and powerful, whilst remaining unresponsive to demands from the global poor. Meanwhile the everyday decisions of citizens of the affluent West can make the lives of the poor still more precarious. Our contribution to climate change is but one, increasingly familiar, example.

We live in a divided world. But many people believe that we can, and must, do better, and that a more just world is possible. Campaign groups, activists, and some of our political leaders have worked hard to raise the profile of a series of important global issues. These range from child labour, to global poverty, to environmental destruction, to the activities of tax havens, to global trade and the effect it has on patterns of prosperity, and much else besides. Global inequality too has repeatedly been identified as a key challenge for the twenty-first century. The United Nations has endorsed a number of 'Sustainable Development Goals' which would, among other things, ensure that extreme poverty is ended in the coming decades, that inequalities both between and within countries are reined back (including, not least, gender inequalities), and that all countries have access to clean water and green energy sources.

At the same time, an extensive academic debate on the meaning and demands of 'global justice' has taken place. It has asked profound questions about how we should live together on our amazing but nevertheless limited planet, what we owe to one another, and how progress towards a more just world can be achieved. Finding answers to these questions has never been more important. Globalization, mass migration, the growth of international trade, and the emergence of global threats such as climate change or pandemics have transformed the background against which we must ask the big political questions of our time. Meanwhile the legacies of slavery and colonialism continue to be felt across the world. But these are large and imposing questions. Indeed, they can appear so enormous that the reader might be forgiven for turning away at the outset. Certainly, achieving justice in a divided world like ours will require more than sticking plasters. But how could a truly just world be achieved?

This book aims to help the reader to think through these hugely important issues. It is organized around three key questions which anyone interested in global justice must grapple with. *What is the problem? Why should you care? And what, if anything, can be done?* In the first chapter, I outline the twin challenges of global poverty and global inequality, and assess how patterns of prosperity have changed over time. But at the same time, I try to go beyond the statistics to show something of the reality of living with severe deprivation.

The second chapter examines the reasons for caring about global justice. It is not hard to see why those at the receiving end of poverty and inequality might care, of course. But most readers of this book will probably, like me, come from relatively wealthy Western countries. I aim to show why global justice should be a major concern for *all* of us. Citizens of developed countries do not, of course, hold all of the answers: global justice must be a partnership between people in rich and poor countries, and we have much to learn by listening to the concerns of people in the developing world. But there is, nevertheless, an important role to be played by ordinary citizens in the West. We may possess more power to effect a more just world than we think – and with that power comes responsibility.

In the final chapter I examine what, if anything, can be done to ease global injustice. I address the question of whether achieving global justice is 'feasible', and sketch a series of key reforms which would move us closer to a just world. I will not attempt to provide a detailed account of what a fully just world would look like. But the reforms I outline would undoubtedly represent important steps on the path towards such a world. Global justice matters, and progress in meeting this most important of contemporary challenges is within our reach.

What is the Problem?

Living in Poverty

At the time of writing, eight hundred million people are living in what the World Bank calls severe poverty.[1] What this means in practice, according to the Bank's definition, is that these millions upon millions of people each have less than $1.90 to live on every day. For many of us, that figure is already unimaginably low – the price of a cup of coffee, more or less. Still, you might be forgiven for thinking that it is perhaps enough for some people to get by. After all, in some countries one or two dollars might buy you a lot. That thought, however, needs to be quickly reconsidered. When the World Bank says that someone is living on the poverty line, it does not mean that he or she actually *has* $1.90 to live on. The World Bank is, understandably, interested in what people can buy with the money they have. When it says that eight hundred million people are living on $1.90 a day, what it actually means is that they have access to no more, and quite possibly much less, than what you could buy with $1.90 *in the contemporary United States*.

Just imagine for a moment what that might mean for a person's daily existence. Someone attempting to live on $1.90 per day in the US would be living on a tiny fraction – less than a fiftieth – of the minimum wage in that country. Their entire existence, in all likelihood, would be devoted to fulfilling their most basic needs. They would go to sleep not knowing whether tomorrow was going to be a day in which they, or their children, would eat. Unsurprisingly, the bulk of the income of the world's severely poor is indeed spent on food, often of poor quality. That leaves, unfortunately, very little for anything else; and for the severely poor, this is a long-term reality. Access to education and healthcare is an ongoing challenge – never mind culture, or travel, or sports or other hobbies. Any unseen contingency – an illness which prevented you from working for a few days, say, or even discovering that your child needs a new pair of shoes – could throw your hand-to-mouth existence into jeopardy. As well as having very low incomes, the global poor have almost nothing in the way of wealth – and hence no safety net against emergencies, and no nest egg with which to nurture dreams for the future.[2]

Eight hundred million people live that kind of existence, day in and day out. As well as lacking access to adequate food, water and housing, their poverty may expose them to social stigma and political exclusion. The poor, all too often, are those who politicians can afford to ignore. Their poverty may expose them to other dangers too. They may be driven to take up any offer of work they can find, even if the work is dangerous, degrading, exploitative or illegal. Most of the world's severely poor are women, and their poverty may place them at the mercy of men who wish to control or abuse them.[3] Many of the poor will face political repression on the basis of their religion or ethnic group. Political exclusion and poverty can come together to form a vicious circle: their poverty, and the need to dedicate so much time to survival, may shut the poor out from opportunities to make their voices heard; their lack of voice in politics may then make it still less likely that the conditions of their life will change for the better. Whether as a result of repression or simply due to grinding poverty, many of the world's poor place their lives in danger by attempting to flee to another country. As the bodies washed ashore on the beaches of the Mediterranean in recent years attest, their flight often exposes them to still further dangers. But even the lucky ones, who arrive safely on foreign shores, may face a precarious, marginalized future in their country of destination.[4]

Poverty, then, is not just a matter of a lack of income. The poor lack not only money – though that certainly matters – but also access to many of the ingredients of a decent life which citizens in the West are able to take for granted. The poor learn from a young age to live with patchy provision of education, especially at a secondary level. They become accustomed to insecure access to even basic healthcare, and frequently face poor quality air and unsanitary living conditions. Even water, that most basic necessity for any human life, exposes the severely poor to considerable dangers. Millions of people across the world suffer from waterborne diseases and from exposure to waterborne toxins such as arsenic. Millions of people – most often women – must spend hours each day locating and transporting fresh water for drinking, cooking and cleaning.[5] When they find it, they often pay a heavy price. The cost of water in Ghana and Papua New Guinea is far higher than in the UK and the US, and can account for a significant proportion of a family's income.[6]

Given that poverty is about more than simply dollar income, it has been argued – with some justification – that the World Bank's $1.90 poverty line is too crude to be truly useful. Perhaps fixating on these income figures deflects our attention from the sheer variety of difficulties people face in leading secure and healthy lives. The economist and philosopher Amartya Sen has argued that what matters is what people are able to *do*: the 'capabilities', as he puts it, that they are able to take for granted in their everyday lives. Core capabilities might include the ability to participate in politics, to learn about the world, and to enjoy good health. Such insights can form the basis of a more multi-faceted notion of human development which moves away from an exclusive focus on measures such as GDP or the purchasing power-adjusted dollar income of the poor.[7] The so-called Multidimensional Poverty Index – which measures access to healthcare and education, as well as basics such as water, electricity and so on – is a leading example.[8] A conception of poverty that moves away from an exclusive focus on income is undoubtedly superior. As a model of poverty gains in complexity, it will no longer deliver such clear messages about trends in global poverty; but as we will see in the final chapter of this book, a more complex model bears dividends when it comes to thinking about the best *responses* to global poverty. If poverty simply means a lack of money, then we might suppose that the obvious remedy is to provide more of it. If poverty also involves political marginalization and inequalities of status, the appropriate solutions must be more complex.

Still, whether we focus on income alone or on a wider range of measures, we confront the fact that the worst-off people in many societies are doing badly on pretty much every score. That is not to downplay the resilience and creativity involved in living in poverty, for the poor must and do become experts in coping with uncertainty, working long hours and seizing any opportunity that comes. But it is to emphasize the odds that the poor are striving against. For the very poor, difficulties which most of us would take in our stride – living, as we do, in societies where basic healthcare and education and some kind of social safety net can still usually be taken for granted – can make the difference between life and death. In many cases the outcome of the daily struggle with poverty *is* death. On average, fifty thousand people die every single day from poverty-related causes.[9] Most of them are children in the first few years of life, who fall prey to illnesses which would be easily remedied if they lived in wealthy countries of the world.

To put that figure into some context, at the end of 2017 the world celebrated a year in which no-one at all had died in commercial jet crashes. This result was a remarkable testament to human skill, sound regulation and technical know-how. Aviation experts and policy-makers rightly patted themselves on the back for such a momentous achievement. But right now, during every day that passes, the equivalent of *fifty* jumbo jets full of people die from poverty-related causes – including conditions such as diarrhoea, measles and pneumonia – many of which are easily preventable. Whereas deaths from spectacular accidents garner extensive media attention, the same cannot be said for deaths from poverty.[10] We have become inured to the existence of poverty, and struggle to see past the poverty statistics to the daily reality of individuals living in poverty.

So, just who are the world's poor? One of the most striking facts is that most of them are female. Worldwide, women work longer hours than men, but earn less, own less and have poorer access to financial services. Older women, and unmarried mothers, are especially vulnerable to poverty, and their poverty can make them more vulnerable in turn to various forms of exploitation.[11] Almost half of the world's poor are children. Among people of working age, roughly two-thirds work in farming. Four out of every five live in the countryside, as opposed to cities.[12] Meanwhile – though it might seem so obvious that it does not need stating – the vast majority of the world's poor are non-white. Patterns of poverty have often been, and remain to this day, highly marked by race or ethnicity. Many of the poor also live in places formerly colonized by Western countries. According to some commentators, colonialism appears to have nipped in the bud the processes of development which have led some countries into prosperity and security.[13]

These figures – and the patterns they illustrate – are instructive and important in their own right. But cascades of statistics do sometimes risk blinding us to the everyday reality of people in severe poverty. For each person in this category, poverty is not a statistic but a way of life. Fortunately, there are now a number of pioneering projects which allow us an insight, however imperfect, into the lives of individual families living in extreme poverty. On the Dollar Street website, for example, many poor families from around the world have volunteered to give an invaluable insight into the places where they live, sleep, cook and work.[14]

Where in the world do the severely poor live? Perhaps the most important thing to note is that very few of them indeed live in the affluent West. Even after recent austerity measures, the poor in the so-called 'developed countries' are typically still able to gain some assistance from the state, whether that means free education, some measure of basic healthcare or, in most cases, some variety of out-of-work benefits. The homeless in Europe and the US are, to be sure, very badly off, and their plight is an affront to any supposedly affluent society.[15] The same can be said of the illegal immigrants and asylum seekers who inhabit the margins of our societies.[16] But if we were to use the World Bank's poverty line to identify the poor in Europe or the US, we would find almost no-one – a small fraction of 1 per cent of the population – living below it. Instead, the overwhelming majority of the world's poor live in what we tend to call the 'developing world'. Many of them live in India, and in other poor states in Asia. But things are changing. Whereas a few decades ago we could state confidently that most of the world's poor lived in Asia, in the twenty-first century severe poverty is coming to be increasingly concentrated in Africa. Many Asian economies have grown rapidly in recent decades, and huge numbers of their citizens have managed to claw their way above the poverty line – though many of them are still much worse off than their counterparts in the West. In much of

Africa, however, this kind of escape has not occurred, and the number of people living in severe poverty has actually increased in recent years.[17] In many places on the continent, progress towards prosperity, peace and opportunity has been non-existent.[18]

The point about trends is important. According to polling evidence, many people in the West believe that the total number of people living in poverty is increasing, or at best stubbornly refusing to budge downwards. This might explain why so many people are pessimistic about tackling the problem. The reality looks quite different, however. According to the World Bank's figures, there have been terrific successes in recent decades when it comes to helping the worst-off escape from poverty. If eight hundred million people live in poverty now, in 1990 the number was approximately two billion.[19] The escape of so many from poverty is a truly remarkable achievement – without question one of the most important changes in the contemporary world. Still, as we have noted, the World Bank's figures give us at best part of the picture. Whilst the situation facing many of the world's poor *has* undoubtedly improved, it is imperative that people's apparent pessimism about world poverty is not quickly replaced by an easy complacency.

Global poverty remains a huge challenge for at least three reasons. First, we have seen that poverty is about more than just income. Even when people manage to claw their way above the Bank's poverty line, they may still face poor access to healthcare, or education, live in dirty or dangerous conditions, face political exclusion, and so on. And this matters. Second, we must remember that the Bank's poverty line is *very* low. It would be a major mistake to assume that, once people manage to escape severe poverty on this definition, we no longer need to worry about their fates. We ought to want to know, for example, how *far* people have managed to move above this poverty line, and how *securely*. Third, as we have just seen, there are many parts of the world where progress has been slow or non-existent. It is scant consolation to *them* that rapid progress has been made elsewhere. In many Western societies, politicians and moral leaders claim that the health or success of a society can be judged by how well it treats its least fortunate. In the US, George W. Bush proudly called his flagship education reform the 'No Child Left Behind' Act. Though the Act itself became mired in controversy, its title at least captured a noble goal. In Britain, likewise, a project to support the wellbeing of vulnerable children was called 'Every Child Matters'. On a global scale too, we ought to see the quality of the lives lived by the poorest of the poor as an important benchmark of human progress. Against that benchmark, we are still failing.

A World of Differences

The situation in which the world's poor must live their lives is all the more striking because elsewhere in the world – periodic recessions aside – so much has improved so fast. The rapid progress which made the lifestyles of citizens of wealthy countries possible is easy to take for granted, but it is important to resist the temptation. In the last century and a half, life expectancy in most parts of the world has soared, not least since many previously deadly communicable diseases have been brought safely under control. People living today are considerably healthier, taller and better nourished than their ancestors from just a few generations back.[20] At the outset of the nineteenth century, perhaps *eight tenths* of the world's population lived in what the World Bank would today define as severe poverty. Within two short centuries that picture changed remarkably, at least for many. Our world's eight hundred million severely poor now represent roughly *one* tenth of the world's population.[21] In the words of a leading economist, the bulk of humanity has, in the bigger picture, only rather recently staged a 'Great Escape' from the miserable conditions it faced for most of human history.[22] Even within living memory, many of us have become used to a nutritious diet, comfortable homes complete with labour-saving devices, foreign travel, efficient transport and many and varied cultural opportunities.

There have been other important changes too. Democracy has spread rapidly, giving ordinary citizens a greater say in the decisions which affect them. Between 1970 and 2000, the number of democratic countries in the world increased from 35 to 120[23] – though the picture in our own century has been more mixed. *Within* democratic countries, the franchise was gradually extended from the upper to the middle and finally to the working classes. Women gained the vote in many countries in the course of the twentieth century, and formal or informal barriers to the participation of ethnic minorities were often removed – though this too represents an unfinished revolution.

Within recent years, however, at least for the younger generations within many Western societies, material progress has come to seem much less certain. Growth rates in developed countries appear to be in long-term decline. In the aftermath of the great recession of 2008, many countries pursued austerity policies which involved large and enduring cuts to important social services. Housing and higher education have come to seem unaffordable for many. Indeed, for the ordinary worker, the problems go back even further than the current period of austerity. When adjusted for inflation, wages for middle-income workers have been more or less stagnant since the 1970s, and wages for those on low incomes have fallen.[24] The share of national income going to labour has fallen in most developed countries, whilst the share going to the owners of capital – our employers – has increased.[25]

At the same time, it is clear that vast wealth is still being created, and many people, even in an age of austerity, have been doing very well indeed. The ranks of the millionaires and even billionaires among us are burgeoning. Many of them have famously become philanthropists, with the personal power to make decisions which will have momentous consequences for hundreds of thousands of lives. But not all of them have turned to charitable endeavours, and many of those who have remain staggeringly wealthy. A glance at a newspaper or magazine rack will provide an insight into the lifestyles of many of the truly rich. The *Financial Times*, for instance, publishes a supplement called 'How To Spend It'. A quick read will give a glimpse into lives characterized by exclusive travel, superyachts, and the struggle to keep on top of the latest movements in the art market.

All of this brings forcefully home that we live in a world not just of enduring *poverty*, but of immense national and global *inequality*. Whereas the global economy is still hugely productive, its fruits are not evenly distributed. As an example, the world saw significant income growth between 1980 and 2016. But the top 1 per cent of earners captured twice as much of that growth as the poorest 50 per cent of the world's population.[26] Indeed, 'the 1 per cent' is now a recognized political category, with movements like Occupy Wall Street claiming to represent the other 99 per cent. Inequality is not a new phenomenon by any means, but as the work of some pioneering economic historians has shown, we live in a world – and in countries – in which wealth, as well as income, has become still more highly concentrated. And those who own great wealth are proving increasingly successful at hanging on to it, and in passing it down the generations. Inherited wealth is making a comeback both nationally and globally, suggesting that, increasingly, our elites are where they are because of their ancestry rather than their own efforts.[27]

To ordinary citizens in wealthy countries, inequality is a major threat. In recent years, very few of the gains from globalization have accrued to the lower and middle classes in developed countries – whilst the wealthy continue to do exceptionally well.[28] For this reason, the struggle against global inequality may deliver dividends for citizens of wealthy countries who wish to reduce the hold of great wealth on their economies and their democracies. Nevertheless, it is important to recognize that the picture when it comes to great inequality is globally quite complex. When we look at the worldwide picture, the 1 per cent are an increasingly global category. The ranks of the 1 per cent have been joined by billionaires from China, India, Nigeria and Latin America. Nevertheless, the numbers from those places

remain relatively small. More than half of the global top
1 per cent are from the US and the UK alone.[29]

Similar points can be made about the top 10 per cent.
Many readers will not be accustomed to thinking of
themselves as part of the top 10 per cent in the global
income rankings. But that is just what many of you will
be. In the United States, fully 60 per cent of the population are in the global top 10 per cent.[30] In fact, even the
poorest American has a higher income than all but the
very wealthiest inhabitants of India.[31] If you are college
educated and in a professional job, then there is a strong
probability that you are close to the top of the global
income hierarchy. The figures for the UK are similar.
In China, by contrast, even after decades of incredible
economic growth, only 2.5 per cent of the population
belong to the global top 10 per cent. In India, the figure
is less than one third of one per cent, or one in three
hundred people. In Nigeria, the figure is a half of 1 per
cent.[32]

This suggests that our country of birth exerts an enormous influence on our prospects in life. In fact, our
country of birth continues to be the most significant
factor in determining how our lives will go. It is a far
bigger determinant of our life chances than our class,
race or gender.[33] Inequalities *between* countries far outstrip inequalities *within* countries. We have seen that
there are major global inequalities when it comes to
income and wealth. But the same can be said when it
comes to consumption. The lifestyles of people in developed countries are hugely more resource-intensive than
those of people living in poor countries. The average
US citizen is responsible for the emission of 16.5 metric
tonnes of carbon dioxide each year. The average citizen

of Chad, Rwanda or Ethiopia is responsible for one tenth of a tonne.[34] It would take 165 people, in those countries, to match the carbon consumption of one US citizen. The average citizen of Canada consumes thirty-seven times as much energy as the average Bangladeshi.[35] Americans, on average, are responsible for five times as much freshwater consumption as someone from the Democratic Republic of the Congo.[36]

Interestingly, whereas there is broad agreement that global inequality rose sharply in the decades leading up to the 1980s, the trends in more recent years are the subject of some controversy.[37] On the one hand, it seems clear that global inequality was bolstered by the progress made in the developed world over the past couple of centuries. In more recent decades, though, inequality has been held back somewhat as countries such as Taiwan, South Korea and China rose in the global income hierarchy. The emergence in China of a substantial middle class has by itself done much to narrow the gap in the middle of the income distribution.[38] If we remove the success of China from the picture, it becomes one of even more rampant inequality, of countless millions mired in poverty and continued rapid gains for the privileged few.

Why are there such massive inequalities? Some readers might wonder whether the great gulfs in prosperity we've been discussing are simply the result of hard work versus laziness, or the making of good rather than bad choices. But it is hard to find the kind of evidence that would support a view like that. To the contrary, the wealthier a country is, the fewer hours its citizens tend to work. The average working week is now thirty-five hours or fewer in countries like Australia, Canada and

France. But in countries like Bolivia, China, Egypt and Turkey, the average is between fifty and sixty hours.[39] If people in developing countries are working an extra three hours every single day of the week – despite an inferior diet, and inferior healthcare – then a lack of effort is probably not the issue. Likewise, we might suspect that people in developing countries are simply less 'productive' than individuals living in rich countries. But the available evidence points in the other direction. When people migrate from poor countries to rich countries, their productivity rapidly rises – suggesting that it is the place they find themselves in, and not their own personal characteristics, which is exerting an influence on their productivity.[40] People in developing countries do, however, face significantly weaker opportunities. Those who seek to 'get on', in the world's poorest countries, will be faced with a lack of physical infrastructure and transport links. They will already have faced far poorer access to education. Millions go without any education at all, and in sub-Saharan Africa fewer than 30 per cent of children ever get to attend secondary school, never mind university.[41] For those who are nevertheless entrepreneurial enough to want to start up their own small businesses, a major obstacle will be access to credit. Credit – that is, the ability to borrow now and repay later – is absolutely crucial to allowing people to escape from deprivation, and to allowing economies as a whole to grow. But especially in rural areas – where most poor people live – access to credit is usually very poor. When it is available, it is often 'informal', and lent at punitive interest rates. Worldwide, two billion people have no access at all to regulated financial services such as banks and credit agencies.[42] Women are systematically less likely to have access to credit (and to have entered formal education) than men.[43]

What about government policy? Showing that the opportunities open to people in the world's poorest country are highly constrained does not prove that these countries bear no responsibility at all for their degree of prosperity. Some countries, after all, have managed to bring millions out of poverty successfully: we have noted the example of East Asian countries, and especially China, already. Politics, and policy, certainly matter. As we will see in the final chapter, the quality of domestic institutions can make a big difference, with good institutions making economic growth and poverty reduction more likely. Societies which are politically 'inclusive', and where the rule of law is respected, appear to have better prospects when it comes to economic development (especially when they are democratic).[44] But does this mean that *individuals* in developing countries can be blamed for their poverty? If they have exercised political power themselves, and wielded it badly, then quite possibly. But things are rarely that simple. First of all, improving the quality of political institutions is no mean feat, especially from a starting-point of grinding poverty. Genuine opportunities for institutional reform may be few and far between.[45] It is also worth remembering that colonialism will have left some countries with national borders and state institutions that claim little allegiance from local populations – something for which locals can hardly be held responsible. Second, we cannot conclude from the success of some that opportunities are available to all. For countries at the bottom of the global income ladder, the only route towards development might involve borrowing money from international lenders, and accepting the policies which come along with those loans – even though the policies recommended by the major lending institutions have often failed to generate sustained growth. Notably, the East Asian countries that have grown rapidly in recent decades tend to have ignored the advice of the International Monetary Fund (IMF) and World Bank and ploughed their own furrow, and have done very well regardless.[46] Other countries may not have that luxury. Indeed, in the present century the opportunities for genuine catch-up development on the part of poor countries might have narrowed further still.[47]

But most important of all, perhaps, is a point about the relationship between individual and collective responsibility. Let's assume that governments in many developing countries have made bad choices, albeit from a fairly narrow set of options. If we want to assess whether people 'deserve' to be rich or poor, what we need to assess is the responsibility of *individual citizens* for the circumstances in which they find themselves. Even in cases where government policy has been frankly wrongheaded in poor countries, individual citizens can scarcely be held responsible for the consequences unless they had a reasonable opportunity to influence that policy. Roughly 40 per cent of the world's population, however, still live in countries which cannot be described as free or democratic even by the most minimal standards, and these people are disproportionately concentrated in developing countries.[48] Many of the poor also live in countries where corruption in government and in public service is rampant.[49] But if citizens lack even minimal influence over political decisions, what they bear responsibility for is not the success or failure of their economies as a whole, but the choices made in their *own* lives. And here the picture of striving hard against unfavourable odds is probably the most accurate one. People born into poverty are frequently resilient, creative and hardworking.[50] They need to be. But the poor performance of their governments is often, from their point of view, just one more misfortune. For children being born into poverty – as thousands are each day – the situation is especially clear. Children may learn to adjust to a meagre start in life. But holding them responsible for their start in life would be an insult. From the point of view of the young, a local history of conflict or poor government, as opposed to peace and good governance, is simple bad luck. People born into the developed world inherit a set of advantages which they learn to take for granted, but which are not the product of their own efforts. Others are less fortunate.

But perhaps the metaphor of good and bad fortune is the wrong one. For, as I will argue in the next chapter, wealthy countries are very good at locking in the advantages their citizens have come to enjoy, whether by excluding immigrants from the poor world, or by using their power within international institutions to advance their own interests. In a provocative analogy, the Canadian philosopher Joseph Carens has likened our contemporary world to a feudal society. In a feudal society, a person's role in life was assigned at birth, and moving from the peasantry to the aristocracy was tremendously difficult. In liberal democratic societies, we tend to be deeply uncomfortable with the idea that our places in society should be based on inheritance. Instead, we congratulate ourselves on having achieved (some degree of) equality of opportunity. But at the same time, perhaps we are complicit in sustaining a world in which our place of birth exerts an influence on our prospects in life which is every bit as powerful as the influence of blood in feudal society.[51]

Local Problems?

Despite great progress in many areas in recent decades, we have seen that there is deep disadvantage in many parts of the world. That is obviously a problem for people in developing countries. But perhaps their disadvantage should be thought of as a local problem, rather than a problem for *us*. It's unfortunate that some people have so much less than we do, we might think, but it's not necessarily something we need to worry too much about. After all, we live, for the most part, in secure and comfortable societies. In the next chapter, I will present several reasons for caring about both poverty and inequality, even if the people at the receiving end live far away from us. But in any case, the response is shortsighted. Poverty and inequality are global problems, not local ones. For one thing, when the global economy works for the few rather than the many, we are all affected. At the same time as the global economy has grown, progress has stalled even for ordinary citizens in wealthy countries. For another thing, global poverty and inequality are bound up together with many of the greatest challenges we face in the world today. Tackling those problems will require us to engage with patterns of prosperity across the world.

To illustrate the point, I will discuss one example here: that of climate change. The vast majority of people – including scientists and ordinary citizens – now accept that climate change threatens to impact on all of our lives, in potentially very serious ways. To be sure, the poor of the world will tend to be hardest hit if dangerous climate change comes to pass. They will be hardest hit for the simple reason that they possess the least capacity to successfully adapt to shocks to their way of life.[52] People with money, when confronted with climate change – whether that means encroaching water, or ever more unpredictable weather patterns, for example – will often have the option to move somewhere safer. People living from day to day on very little will have far fewer options. They will not have the money required to move house, or even up sticks and look for employment elsewhere. They may rely on families and broader networks which are hard to move.

But as well as amplifying the *effects* of climate change, gulfs in income and wealth make *tackling* climate change in the first place much harder. To see why, it's worth taking a step back and thinking about what kind of problem climate change is. It's such a familiar problem, especially to younger generations, that this might appear unnecessary. But it's nevertheless worth doing, because we might be mistaken about the kind of problem that climate change poses for us. So, let's begin at the beginning. Climate change is, broadly speaking, what happens when fossil fuels are burned for energy – releasing carbon dioxide and other greenhouse gases into the atmosphere – and when trees, which whilst in the soil lock huge quantities of carbon safely into the ground, are cut down (the effects are especially dramatic when they are burned). The solution to climate change is, quite simply, to find alternative energy sources – whether this means wind power, solar or wave power, or something else – and to stop cutting down trees (and, ideally, to replant deforested areas while we're at it).

Given that we have been aware of these processes for decades, we might be tempted to ask: why hasn't humanity, with all of its technical ingenuity, found alternative sources of energy yet? The answer is that we have. We already have the ability to make extremely efficient solar panels and wind turbines. Recent years have provided striking evidence of that: China has recently cancelled construction of scores of new coal-burning power stations, for instance, and it has been able to do so because wind and solar power can now be provided even more cheaply.[53] So why is climate change *still* a problem? Why doesn't everyone simply roll out renewable technologies, and wind down the fossil fuel industry? One political reason is that fossil fuel industries still exert a regrettable hold on government in many countries, extracting subsidies which make them artificially competitive.[54] Those subsidies should be switched immediately to renewable technologies en masse, and in time even those subsidies should become unnecessary.

But another reason is that many countries simply cannot afford to make the switch to green energy. The people of Chad, one of the least-developed countries in Africa, might love to roll out solar panels and wind turbines to drive much-needed industrialization. But doing so requires not only technical know-how, but large amounts of capital. And capital is something many African countries lack. In the meantime, those countries turn to whatever sources of energy they can find – which in many cases means coal, which is both the most carbon-intensive fuel source we know of, and one which, because of the fumes that arise from burning it, is associated with terrible public health problems. There is plenty of money in the global economy with which to roll out renewables. But from the point of view of tackling climate change, it is in the wrong place.

In fact, we have a classic stand-off. Rich countries quite rightly point out that the world cannot afford for poor countries to industrialize along the same dirty, carbon-intensive path they pursued themselves. Poor countries quite rightly point out that, pressing problem though climate change is, their own endemic poverty demands their attention. And as it stands, industrializing as fast as they can – even if this means dirty and dangerous industrialization – appears to be the best way to make progress. The solution is obvious to many: rich countries ought to share their technology with poor countries, and help fund its rollout across the developing world. Climate change is a pressing global problem, but it is not one which the poor should pay to fix. It is not, for that matter, a problem they created, and it is not a problem they can much afford to bear the costs of fixing either. To that end, a number of mechanisms have been put in place – including the UN's Green Climate Fund – to fund the rollout of clean energy technology. Such projects are, for the most part, chronically under-funded, as rich countries have either refused to commit sufficient funds, or failed to deliver on what they have committed. But the principle is the right one: as a global problem, climate change demands a global solution. And the solution cannot be to load the costs of dealing with the problem onto the shoulders of countries which are already dealing with a major problem of their own: severe poverty. What this tells us is that the problem of climate change and the problem of poverty are deeply intertwined, and that there can be no prospect of dealing with the first problem without dealing with the second one too. No solution to the climate quandary can stick – no international agreement will be accepted by the poor of the world, and quite rightly so – unless it simultaneously addresses the development needs of the poorest of our world.

Conclusion

This chapter has given a brief insight into the extent of global poverty in the twenty-first century. The fight against severe poverty is unfinished business, and in the rest of this book we will examine some ways in which people in the rich world might be making the problem worse, as well as some ways in which they can make it better. One thing which is striking about severe poverty is that it exists in the midst of such incredible affluence – affluence which would have been hard to imagine a few centuries ago, but which many of us now take for granted. We live in a world which exhibits not only crushing poverty, but also tremendous inequality. Rather than being problems 'for the poor', we have noted that global poverty and inequality may be bound up with other pressing global problems that we face, and make those problems harder to solve. In the next chapter, we will look more systematically at the reasons we have for objecting to poverty and inequality at the global level, before investigating the remedies open to us in the final chapter.

2

Why Should You Care?

The Globalization of Concern

If you are leading a relatively comfortable life in a wealthy industrialized country, why should you care if others thousands of miles away are faring less well? What does it matter to you? Why *should* it matter?

We probably all know people who will confidently declare that our only concern should be our nearest and dearest, and that how people in other countries get by is their business and not ours. One of the most remarkable features of political life in recent decades, though, is that voters, and the leaders they elect, have become less and less confident that such an attitude is acceptable. Our understanding of global issues – such as poverty, or war, or migration or climate change – has increased enormously. We are now aware, if we were not before, that we live in a global economy, and that the products we consume, or play with, or wear, are produced within complex global supply chains. We appreciate that the decisions that our governments take – whether to increase or cut taxes, whether to encourage investment in one industry or another – are informed by the knowledge that other leaders in other countries will be making similar decisions of their own. Like it or not, we are aware that we face problems – pandemics, or global warming, or terrorism – which will not be solved unless we learn to cooperate with people in distant places.

This is not to say that we have given global issues as much attention as they deserve. Politicians are all too focused on the next election, and making the world a fairer place does not always look like a vote-winner when local interest groups can shout very loud indeed. But the view that we should be thinking not only as national citizens but also, in some sense, as 'citizens of the world' has grown in force. When US President Donald Trump announced that he was taking the US out of the Paris Climate Agreement, the reaction from the rest of the world was one of shock (how can you abdicate your global responsibilities?), swiftly followed by determination (if the US is not going to lead, the rest of us will).

Within philosophy, a similar shift in focus has taken place. When philosophers asked questions about the meaning of justice, or about how much inequality there should be, or about the duties the wealthy might have towards the poor, they assumed until very recently that these were questions about *social* justice: about the demands of justice within a single society, conceived of as a more or less closed system in which people cooperate together in order to advance the greater good. That was very much the view of John Rawls, for instance – the most famous scholar of justice of the last century.[1] There was, to be sure, a great tradition of thinking about justice stemming from earlier times, when the pre-eminent unit of political life was not the nation-state, but the city-state or even the empire. But in recent centuries, questions about justice came to be associated more or less exclusively with the problem of how a national community was going to govern itself. Karl Marx may have claimed that working men of the world had no country, that our interest in the overthrow of capitalism was a common global interest which necessitated a global revolution. And Virginia Woolf may have declared that 'As a woman I have no country'; but these 'internationalist' voices were rather lonely ones.[2] Even at the turn of our present century, many philosophers assumed that justice was something fellow citizens owed to one another, via the institutions of their state.[3]

In recent years, however, it has become less and less clear how such an exclusive focus on justice within the nation-state can be defended. Why would we assume that the single society is in some sense the container for justice? What would justify that assumption?

One quite common idea is that societies are characterized by particularly intense forms of interaction. Citizens cooperate with each other in order to advance common goals – such as securing a productive economy, or maintaining law and order. The ties that bind citizens are more intense, and have a much greater impact on how their individual lives go, than the much looser ties they share with outsiders. The institutions which make the greatest difference to our everyday lives, it might be pointed out, are those of our own state, rather than more far-flung global institutions. So perhaps our focus should be on getting these local institutions right. Perhaps this is what justice means: making sure that the institutions of our society operate fairly, treating citizens (but not necessarily outsiders) with equal concern and respect. The argument can loosely be called a 'statist' one, because it suggests that when we think about justice, the major challenge is to make sure that the institutions of our own state are functioning properly (that is, fairly). The demands of justice at the global level, by contrast, are much more modest.[4]

But there seems to be a powerful response to any argument along these lines.[5] There is now a *global* economy, along with a set of rules and institutions which have arisen to govern it. The ties that bind us as citizens may still have a major impact on our life chances, but the great bountifulness of our economies depends to a substantial degree upon global cooperation.[6] A country like the UK is not self-sufficient; it imports more than half of its food,[7] and half of its energy,[8] as well as exporting many goods and services. The world economy more broadly depends upon dizzying movements of key resources such as metals, minerals and oil – as well as information and ideas. Unnoticed by most, our economies are underpinned by enormous 'virtual' transfers of water – water, that is, which is used elsewhere in the production of the food and energy we consume.[9]

If our consumption depends upon the efforts of distant outsiders, the same can be said for production. A Hollywood movie executive deciding which film to make no longer makes that call based on expected receipts in US movie theatres alone. He or she makes that decision by estimating *global* receipts. The decision to make one movie rather than another is at least partly grounded on the assumption that there is a global audience out there and that, by and large, overseas audiences will observe the intellectual property rights of the movie studio (they will pay for their tickets, and the agreed proportion of receipts will then flow back to the studio). The specialization which international trade makes possible has hugely improved the efficiency of the global economy, boosting the sheer weight of outputs. And international trade has rules, which are overseen by major international institutions such as the World Trade Organization and the International Labor Organization (which ensure that some version of property rights, and some – relatively thin – version of labour standards, are observed by all members). These institutions have mission statements – to bring down barriers to world trade, to spread the benefits of prosperity – though they are not always successful in achieving their goals. The rules they adopt are negotiated internationally by our leaders, and the results can be enormously consequential. As trade barriers are worn down – albeit selectively, and in a piecemeal fashion – some industries fade away, many jobs are 'relocated', and hopefully new opportunities arise. The enormous machinery of international trade – the ports, the container ships and the rules and institutions which oversee them – have not arisen by accident. They have arisen because trade produces great wealth, and a reversion to insular self-sufficiency would be in no-one's interests, especially given the pressing global problems we face. Still, it is legitimate – indeed vital – to ask where the benefits of the global economy are flowing. There are fruits to global cooperation, and the question of what would count as a fair distribution of these spoils is a hugely important one.[10] The global economy, like the domestic economy, can run fairly or unfairly, justly or unjustly. These words are not out of place; they are vital ideas for assessing whether our world is working for the many or for the few. This suggests that the conversation about justice too ought to be globalized.[11]

Times of crisis can make the entanglement of our fates especially plain. The global financial crisis of 2008 may have been caused by dubious dealing in the US mortgage market, but its effects were felt everywhere. It brought down governments (as in Iceland), impoverished many, generated massive debts, and provided a justification for various assaults on the welfare state. The financial world is still deeply globalized, and scarcely any more regulated than it was before the crash, and trends within it exert a powerful influence on patterns of prosperity in the world at large. We are also rapidly learning about the global impacts of our individual consumption decisions. If you live a carbon-intensive life, you may be contributing to the catastrophe of dangerous climate change: you may be helping to cause extreme weather patterns elsewhere in the world, for example, or making the submersion of small island states that bit more likely. If you contribute to plastic pollution, you may be harming, in some small way, the livelihoods of poor fishermen in far-flung countries (as well as marine life itself).[12] The justice-for-single-societies approach now looks hopelessly dated.

Still, it is not only because of the existence of a global economy, or the urgency of common global problems, that the focus on justice within single societies should be rejected. A second and much simpler argument focuses not on the nature of the global economy, but on our shared nature as human beings.[13] After all, despite our many differences, we have a good deal in common. We all need food to eat and fresh water to drink. We all share in the desire to live in a safe and secure environment, and we all have plans and projects which can only reliably be advanced if we are able to exert at least some degree of control over the decisions which affect our lives. Morally, our lives ought to be seen as having equal weight. If we were designing a world from scratch, we ought to design a world which gave people more or less equal prospects of living good lives – of enjoying wellbeing – regardless of their location. When refashioning our institutions and our practices – which is much more common – we ought to be guided by the same principle. It is hard to see how any other principle would treat people with equal respect. A proposal to treat those closest to us as morally more important would fail this basic test. For some, to be sure, this thought will be jarring. For we are used to treating those nearer to us as more important. But it is hard to see what would *justify* that approach.

There might conceivably be good *practical* reasons for focusing on those closer to us. If, for instance, a world where we all looked after those closest to us turned out to be more effective in protecting people's wellbeing than a world in which we had to try to advance everyone's wellbeing at once, then we might be justified in preferring that world. But that would be a practical point, and not a moral one. It would be compatible with treating everyone's interests as equally important in a moral sense. In any case, the key point to note here is that a system in which we helped those closer to us could only be justified if it was *actually* the best way of making sure that everyone's interests were protected.[14] In our world, that's highly unlikely to be the case, for two reasons. First, we face large-scale problems (such as climate change and other environmental problems, terrorism and pandemics) which cannot effectively be dealt with in anything other than a global fashion. And second, many communities have far weaker capacity to advance the wellbeing of their citizens, and some have far greater capacity. In some places in the world, states are more or less wholly ineffective in protecting their citizens, often through no fault of those citizens. In these imperfect circumstances, showing equal concern for the lives of all demands that we take on obligations towards outsiders too. For that reason, some philosophers have thought that familiar ideas about justice can be extended to the global level. Take a much-cherished idea like equality of opportunity, which tends to be endorsed by people on both the left and the right of politics. The ideal of equality of opportunity demands, roughly speaking, that the jobs we end up with, or the wages we earn, depend on our own efforts, and not on irrelevant factors such as our sex, race or class. We could be satisfied that we lived in an equal-opportunity society when, and only when, similarly talented people who happened to be born into different ethnic groups, male or female, from working-class or middle-class backgrounds, had roughly equal prospects of success in life. It would be unjust, by contrast, for people of one class, or sex or ethnicity to face systematically inferior prospects.

But that powerful thought – which is familiar from John Rawls's theory of justice within the state – invites a further one. The point about our race, class or sex is that we do not choose them, and are therefore not responsible for them. It might be acceptable for our lives to go better or worse because of the decisions we make, or the effort we put into our work or training. But to face worse prospects because of irrelevant factors like race or sex seems perverse. But then, we might ask, why would place of birth be any different?[15] After all, none of us chooses which society we happen to be born into. Isn't it therefore every bit as unjust if people born in different countries, with similar abilities and similar willingness to put those talents to work, end up with vastly different prospects?[16]

In the end, both of these arguments point in much the same direction. The first claims that principles of global justice have become relevant because our lives are increasingly bound up together, and because we face common problems which require global solutions. The second claims that principles of global justice are required because we are all human beings, whose lives matter equally.[17] Either way, the assumption that, when we talk about justice, what we are discussing is what citizens of single societies owe to one another looks like an idea whose time is up. Global justice is on the agenda, and rightly so.

Charity, Justice and Rights

Perhaps, having read the last section, you are persuaded that justice cannot begin and end at home, and that we do have some kinds of duties to people on the other side of the world. There is still room for disagreement, though, about what those duties look like. What exactly do we owe to people in other countries?

Here, two distinctions are useful. The first contrasts negative and positive duties. The second contrasts duties of justice with duties of charity.

Let's begin with the distinction between negative and positive duties. Negative duties are, at their simplest, duties not to hurt or impose harms on other people. People tend to believe that they have a moral responsibility not to kill others. Whilst doing so is sometimes permissible, the constraints on killing are very tight (think of cases of self-defence, or cases where a soldier or a policewoman can justly use lethal force to prevent an attacker killing innocent civilians). But negative duties, at heart, ask us *not* to treat people in certain ways, and the embargo on killing people is just one example. International law tells us that we have a legal duty, for instance, not to emit noxious substances that would damage the environment in neighbouring countries.[18] We might also have moral duties not to exploit people in certain ways, or to benefit from their exploitation by others. For instance, perhaps we have a duty not to buy goods which we know are produced in sweatshops using child labour. We may also have a moral duty not to aid in the oppression of citizens in other countries, for instance by selling weapons to brutal dictators.[19] In all of these cases, we will have a duty to take reasonable steps to avoid either causing, or being complicit in, significant harms that might befall other people.

Philosophers tend to agree that when it comes to observing our negative duties, we are not allowed to 'discount' the interests of outsiders.[20] If killing a fellow citizen would be wrong, then killing a foreigner would be equally wrong. If we believe that child labour should be outlawed at home, we probably ought to believe that it should be outlawed abroad too, and to refuse to participate in practices which make it possible. We must take care, in short, to avoid harming outsiders, and we ought to scrutinize our own actions to make sure that we are not encouraging or facilitating harms caused by other people. Distance, in these cases, does not make any moral difference.

But while negative duties are very important, a full account of global justice will also describe the *positive* duties we have towards outsiders. Positive duties are responsibilities to do, or provide, something important for other people. The duty not to take food away from the starving is a negative duty, but the duty to *give* food to the starving is a positive one. It requires deliberate action, rather than mere inaction. Beyond providing relief to the malnourished, taking justice seriously requires us to accept a broader duty to support the economic development of people living in poor countries – to safeguard the conditions, that is, in which they can escape from their present disadvantage.[21] Acting on that duty will likely generate some cost for us. This seems to make positive duties distinctive – for in some cases, negative duties can be observed without imposing any great cost. After all, it is not typically expensive to refrain from killing people. But it seems likely that positive duties will *always* involve some costs, whether in terms of time, or money, or other resources. In the next section, we will consider how these costs ought to be shared out.

A second distinction is also important. Let's stick for now with our question about positive duties. Imagine that Paul is starving, and that we possess food which would allow him to recover. Many people will readily accept, at least in a simple case like this, that we have a duty to give Paul some food. But there might be room for disagreement about what *kind* of duty this is. Many of us believe that we have some kind of moral duty to give to charity. But we also, often, see the exercise of that duty as a matter for our conscience alone. It might be good to give to charity, but if you choose not to, nobody should be able to force you to. Duties of justice, however, are not like this. Duties of justice are typically matched by *entitlements*, or rights. In our example, we might believe that Paul has a *right* – perhaps a human right – to adequate nutrition. If so, and if I am the only person who can help, I don't seem to have a choice in the matter (unless, perhaps, I am starving myself). I *ought* to give Paul some food, and if I refuse to do so, I am keeping from him something to which he is entitled. In the same way, the idea that efforts to improve the situation of the world's poor are basically optional fails to show sufficient respect for the lives – and the entitlements – of people living in poverty.[22] Increasingly, developing-world social movements have themselves adopted the language of rights to emphasize their own agency, and to displace the idea that they are passive victims of injustice, or passive recipients of help.[23] If one has a right to something, it ought to be guaranteed, rather than being left to the discretion of those with greater resources.[24]

Because duties of justice often (if not always) match up with entitlements that people have, it makes much more sense to think of them as being enforceable, at least in principle. If someone decides not to give to charity, the idea that we could permissibly force them to would strike many as odd. But it would be much less odd to believe that people can be obliged to fulfil their duties of justice. If we believe Paul has a right to eat, for example, then we might be prepared to accept that a bystander could oblige me to give him some of my food, or even that he would be justified in taking some himself if I refused to share with him.[25] Within our own societies, we live comfortably with the idea that we have duties of justice; if our neighbour refuses to pay his taxes, we would not be surprised if the tax collector confiscates some of his property, or even carts him off to prison. Indeed, we might think that is exactly what *should* happen. This is, presumably, because the state engages in important activities that it needs tax revenues in order to fund. Our taxes pay for schools and hospitals and roads and courts and a police force. These services are so important that citizens are entitled to expect them. The claim made by supporters of the idea of global justice is that outsiders can have important entitlements too, which impose duties on people the world over. To talk of global justice, as opposed to charity, is to invoke a serious bit of moral language. For supporters of global justice, this is as it should be.

Here's an example. In 2017, the charity Global Justice Now argued that we need to change the way we think about foreign aid. Rather than a charitable endeavour, we should think of aid payments as being much like the regular payments (such as welfare benefits or tax credits) which governments make to some citizens, and which they legitimately come to expect as a matter of right.[26] Now, there are lively debates about the role and future of foreign aid as a vehicle for global justice. As we will see in the next chapter, foreign aid might not even be the most important means we have for promoting the development of poor countries. But the basic point is a sound one. If we are serious about the language of global justice, we need to learn to stop thinking of the things we do for the less advantaged of the world as subject to this kind of discretion, according to which we are able to decide what to give, when, and to whom, and the recipient is obliged to accept the reality of that one-sided relationship. Indeed, this should not be a surprise. There were very good reasons why Western societies replaced private charity with public welfare systems from the nineteenth century onwards. If citizens are owed assistance as a matter of right, then what they receive should not be contingent on the whims of philanthropists and their pet projects. When social assistance is public and predictable, people are able to go about their lives free from the insecurity, and the need to curry favour, which often accompany the charitable relationship. We ought to think about global justice in the same way.[27] The project of securing justice in our world is not optional or negotiable in the way we might think that giving to charity is. It too generates binding entitlements and binding duties. It also means that we should see everyone involved as agents, rather than passive recipients. Delivering on global justice should mean a partnership between the rich and the poor, rather than a top-down process in which all the key decisions are made by the powerful.

The Goal(s) of Global Justice: Reducing Poverty and Inequality

You might be convinced by now – or so I hope – that talk of global justice is more than mere hot air. You might also be willing to entertain the idea that we have duties of justice towards people in far-flung countries, and that those duties will plausibly be both positive and negative in character. But to work out just how demanding those duties are going to be, we need to say a bit more about what the *goals* of global justice are. Here, too, there is room for disagreement.

The last chapter emphasized two key points about the world we live in. The first is that for many people the chances of obtaining even the most basic ingredients of a good life are still very poor. Disease, violence, pollution and exploitation are ever-present threats for hundreds of millions of people. Even in the face of the incredible resilience and creativity that poor people must and do display, life can be perilous and degrading.

The second key point is that our world displays enormous gulfs in life chances. People in developed countries have made huge strides in recent decades, but the forces which have enriched us have left many people in the world far behind. As a result, our place of birth exerts a powerful influence on our prospects of leading a rewarding and healthy life. Rather than being some historical accident, in many cases patterns of prosperity today are depressingly consistent with patterns of prosperity in the past. They continue to bear the traces, for instance, of historical injustices such as imperialism and colonialism. To be sure, not everyone in the wealthy West has enjoyed continual improvements in living standards. In recent decades life has become much more precarious for many people in rich countries too, at the same time as the richest of the rich seem to be pulling out of sight in the race for ever-greater wealth and income. For that reason, ordinary citizens in rich countries and in poor countries might have a degree of common cause in the struggle against the ever-increasing inequality which blights all of our lives. Still, we should be honest enough to recognize that the challenges faced by the typical citizen from an industrialized country and the challenges faced by an inhabitant of one of the world's least advantaged countries are usually very, very different. A typical citizen of one of the world's poorest countries may not have a vote; may have to walk for miles to receive even basic healthcare; may have little choice but to accept work which is dirty or dangerous, if he or she is lucky enough to find work at all. Even after years of austerity and wage stagnation, most of the readers of this book will not live in such precarious circumstances. If you live in a developed country – in Europe, or the US or Canada, in Australia, or New Zealand, say – we have seen that you are probably nested in the top 10 per cent of the world's income ladder, or thereabouts. You are certainly very unlikely to be amongst the ranks of the world's severely poor. To the contrary, you will have learned to take for granted secure access to clean water, electricity, what to our ancestors would have been a bewildering variety of food, and a constant supply of new films, books and music. For many people in the developing world, all of this is a pipe-dream. Though a fortunate few from countries like China, India and Nigeria have joined the ranks of the richest of the rich – the top 1 per cent by income, say – the world distribution of income and wealth remains highly skewed according to nationality. The single fact which explains most of the variation in life chances across the world is still our country of birth.

The question is which of these points we ought to be concerned about. A concern for poverty is a worry about what we might call *absolute* disadvantage – about the fact that some people in the world are doing badly by anyone's standards. A concern for inequality is a worry about *relative* disadvantage – about the fact that some people are doing *worse* than others, and some better. Scholars of global justice tend to agree that absolute disadvantage merits our urgent attention. We surely have both positive and negative duties towards the world's poor, to help them escape poverty and to avoid contributing to their poverty in the first place. As such, the great proclamations of universal basic human rights in the years following the Second World War are to be celebrated. But scholars disagree about whether we should *also* be concerned about relative advantage. Would a just world be one in which severe poverty had been banished? Or would it be one in which the rampant inequalities we can see in the world around us had also been pegged back?

One widespread view is what I would call a 'minimalist' one. This holds that the goal of global justice is to lift everybody above a basic minimum, so that wherever in the world a person lives, her access to the most indispensable ingredients of a life of minimal dignity would be secure.[28] This would mean that everyone, everywhere, had access to sufficient food and clean water to get by, to clothing and housing of a decent standard, and so on. That idea is well captured by the idea that we have basic human rights to, amongst other things, 'subsistence'.[29] Wealthy countries might well have a duty to offer positive assistance to countries which are struggling to get by, so that the basic human rights of their citizens were secure. But once we had achieved that goal, we would have no reason of justice for caring if some countries – and their citizens, of course – happened to be wealthier than others. A world of great inequalities in life prospects which mapped onto our country of birth could still be a just one, so long as everyone was able to get by.[30]

Another, rival, view holds that facts about *unequal* prospects in life *also* matter from the point of view of justice. This position is better described as 'egalitarian', because it focuses on reducing inequality in its own right.[31] There is something objectionable, on this second view, about the fact that some people have *more*, and others have *less*, often for reasons outside of their control. This doesn't mean that we should place any less emphasis on eradicating severe poverty as soon as possible. Anyone who cares about inequality ought to see the improvement of the lot of the world's poor as an urgent priority. But on this second view, easing the lot of the poor is not enough. We could eradicate severe deprivation and still live in an unjust world, if some people were able to lead comparatively luxurious lives whilst others had access to more meagre opportunities. The struggle for global justice is necessarily a struggle against excessive inequality, and not only against poverty.[32]

The debate between the two views continues to rage within scholarly debates on global justice. There is widespread agreement that tackling severe poverty and exclusion ought to be a priority, and this idea is well captured in the advocacy of basic human rights. But whilst the human rights movement has achieved remarkable successes, reining back the power of tyrants and giving succour to the oppressed the world over, the advocacy of human rights is not enough to secure justice.[33] There are several powerful reasons for focusing on both poverty *and* inequality – and hence for adopting the egalitarian view. First and foremost, tolerating massive inequalities is very difficult, if not impossible, to square with the idea that our lives have equal moral worth. As human beings, we all have interests and desires, and plans and projects that we want to advance. Massive inequality means that some of us will have systematically worse prospects of living a secure, healthy and peaceful life. It means that we will have wildly different chances of being able to pursue the things that matter to us in life, whether that be interacting with a healthy natural environment, having children and nurturing them safely into adulthood, engaging in meaningful work, participating in the political life of our community, or a whole host of things besides. Arguments that we ought to *do* something about global poverty – and arguments for the existence of universal human rights – gain much of their force by appealing to shared human capacities – capacities which can be endangered by lives of severe deprivation. When people are very poor, they are much less able to plan for their future, to engage with others in healthy relationships, find a voice in political life, and so on.[34] But if the inability of some to lead fulfilling, healthy lives is an affront to our moral consciences, why isn't the fact that some people, often through no fault of their own, face far inferior prospects? It is not obvious, to say the least, why our concern for people's prospects fades away once they manage to fight their way over some notional poverty line.

An interesting thought experiment would be to imagine yourself discussing the question with one of the world's poor. Picture, if you will, a girl, Asha, on the brink of adulthood. If you could talk to her, she might well want to know *why* her chances in life should be so much worse than yours. It cannot be her fault, after all. Even if you happen to think that poor countries are largely poor because their leaders have made bad decisions or are corrupt, say, that cannot be *her* fault.

Asha has not yet had the chance to shape her country's future. Indeed, she might live in a country where she will probably never get that chance. In a world of mass communication, she may be aware of the kinds of professions that are open to people in a developed country. Perhaps she herself nurtures dreams of becoming a pilot, or an engineer. As the conversation progresses, you might find yourself having to let her down gently. Her ambitions seem a distant prospect, after all. You might explain to her how many obstacles stand in the way of fulfilling an ambition like that. But how could you *justify* the relatively meagre prospects she faces in her life? Or the greater prospects you enjoy in your own, come to that? It is hard to see what would count as a good answer here. You might claim that the wealth of your country is the fruit of years of hard work and sound decision-making, and that it would not be fair if you were asked to share those fruits with people who are not part of your society. That too would be a difficult argument to make. For one thing, as we have seen, the wealth of nations is increasingly bound up with what goes on in a *global* economy. Climate change has further undermined the myth of a world of separate societies determining their own fates. So too does a recognition of the historical record of colonialism, which enriched many and impoverished others. The argument might work, perhaps, if countries were isolated and self-sufficient; but that is not our world, and neither should it be. For another thing, the prosperity of our own societies has deep roots – in all likelihood, it is to a substantial extent built on the back of social and physical capital built up by many generations (and it is well to remember, here, that during many of those generations our ancestors ruled over many other parts of the earth, extracting wealth from them as they did so). But it is hard to see how we, the current generation, can claim any credit for that. From our point of view, the infrastructure in a country like ours looks like a tremendous windfall. People born into the poorest countries of the world, by comparison, are blessed with hugely inferior economic infrastructure and much less in the way of valuable capital. It seems as though they have been dealt a much worse hand in life than us, but it is hard to see how they can be held responsible for that fact.

These arguments suggest that global inequality is wrong in itself. It seems simply unfair for how well our lives go to hinge on facts of geography. But this is not the only reason we might have for objecting to inequality. Inequalities can also be objectionable because of their *effects*.[35] Though it may feel 'normal' to many of us, it is important to pause to consider the consequences of living in a world of massive inequality. One consequence is that our shared institutions become much more responsive to the preferences of the rich, and much less responsive to the poor. In some international institutions, this kind of political inequality is all but hardwired: under a 'gentleman's agreement', the leaders of the World Bank and the IMF, for example, are chosen by the US and the EU. In both institutions, decision-making power is also heavily influenced by each country's gross domestic product (GDP), meaning that the richest countries are hugely over-represented relative to their population size. In the World Trade Organization, decision-making is formally fair – but the real negotiations do not take place in official meetings, but in parallel discussions dominated by the major powers. Poorer countries, with little to offer the rich economies, tend to find their concerns side-lined. As a result, the long-promised 'pro-development' round of trade reforms has never materialized. Instead, trade deals are increasingly agreed bilaterally between powerful countries or blocs – such as the US, EU or China – rather than globally. The poorest of the poor are not party to those agreements, and hence do not benefit from further liberalization of the world economy. Institutions like the IMF and World Bank have, meanwhile, recommended a set of policies for developing countries – including privatization, rapid labour-market liberalization, and the signing of bilateral investment treaties – which have often turned out to do very little for ordinary citizens in those countries. They have, though, been very lucrative for domestic elites and multinational corporations.

In a sense, none of this should surprise us. Within our own countries, we know that the rich can bend the ear of politicians, and the votes of the poor can be taken for granted. We might hope, of course, that institutions can be put in place which are capable of shutting the influence of wealth out of politics. But there are few signs that the influence of wealth on politics is abating. In the meantime, tackling economic inequalities might be the best way of preserving democracy, in our national institutions and in global institutions too.

A further harmful effect of massive inequality is that major global problems become harder to resolve. And the more unequal we become, the greater the obstacles to success. One of these problems is global poverty itself. Even those who focus on easing global poverty alone must recognize that sweeping global inequality can place solutions to poverty further from reach, for instance by rendering international institutions which might hold the solutions unresponsive to the interests of the global poor.[36] In the last chapter I discussed the important example of climate change. Here, the legitimate development aspirations of the less advantaged need somehow to be squared with an effective international solution. At present, wealthy countries have proven themselves more concerned with preserving their advantages than staving off the risk of climate catastrophe. But there are many other problems (including global health epidemics and terrorism) where those who seek to achieve effective international cooperation must face the fact that developing countries have pressing problems of their own – not least endemic poverty – and may have few resources to devote to effective solutions. Those who can afford to pay, meanwhile, find ways to avoid doing so. A somewhat neglected problem where the same dynamic occurs is that of conservation. Within our world, there are many precious resources which we all have a stake in protecting. As luck would have it, often those resources are located in developing countries which are engaged in their own struggles for economic development. All too often, the approach of the international community is simply to urge local communities to preserve these resources, even if it means giving up on development opportunities. But this is inadequate. If there is a global interest in conservation, then the costs of conservation ought to be shared globally, rather than simply being left wherever they fall. Within the conservation community, it is increasingly recognized that underdevelopment and conservation are problems that are intimately connected, and need to be tackled together.[37] If existing development paths involve whole-sale environmental destruction, then the international community will have to help open up alternative, less destructive development paths for the world's poor. Until we do so, local people will continue to face a tragic choice between poverty and environmental destruction.[38]

All of this suggests that many other problems accompany great inequality. It is worth pausing, therefore, to put the case more positively. If inequality corrodes democracy and makes collective problems harder to resolve, then greater equality should have the opposite effect. At the level of nation-states, we have abundant evidence that more equal societies are happier, healthier and more democratic, as well as suffering from less in the way of violence, crime and drug addiction.[39] There is every reason to hope that a more equal world will also be one with less conflict, with greater potential for genuinely democratic decision-making, and more effective cooperation in tackling the common problems we face.

For all of these reasons, my view is that the goal of global justice cannot only be to eradicate severe poverty. It must also be to rein back the huge inequalities that characterize our world. If our lives have equal moral weight, then we ought to have more or less equal prospects in life. It is unfair in its own right if some people are condemned to living with less simply because they are born into communities which are relatively disadvantaged, or where ordinary citizens are relatively powerless when it comes to shaping the nature of the world around them. But inequality will also make many of the common problems we face considerably more difficult to confront effectively. If we do succeed in reining in rampant inequality, then we have every reason to believe that the future will be a happier and more peaceful world, as well as a fairer one.

Making Sacrifices:
Capacity and Contribution to the Problem

In the next chapter we will examine what might be *done* to ease global injustice. Some of the changes we might make could be beneficial for the advantaged as well as the less advantaged, especially if they help to bring about a more peaceful, cooperative world. But most of these changes are going to involve costs to someone. Conceivably, these could involve both financial sacrifices and commitments of what is often our most precious resource: time. This gives rise to an important question: if there are going to be costs involved in bringing about a more just world, who ought to bear them? In this section I will discuss two factors which look like being relevant when we allocate the costs of acting to reduce injustice: our capacity to make sacrifices, and our role in bringing about the injustices we are trying to tackle.[40]

Capacity to help

When we face an urgent problem, it often makes sense to ask those who *can* step forward to help to do so. Those who cannot afford to shoulder the cost of dealing with a problem should not be required to; but those who can afford to should contribute. Moreover, the greater our capacity to absorb sacrifices, the greater a share of the costs we ought to bear. We can call this the 'ability to pay' principle.

This principle is not, in fact, particularly mysterious. It is the reason we standardly ask high-earners to pay more tax than low-earners. It is the reason many countries operate an income tax threshold, so that people on very low incomes are not required to give up *any* of their wages to fund government services. Not only do states often require high-earners to pay more; they usually ask high-earners to give up a greater *proportion* of their income than low-earners. This reflects a judgement that losing £100 will mean a great deal to someone earning £200 a week, but far less to someone earning £1,000 a week. The higher our incomes, the less difference a given financial sacrifice will tend to make to our overall wellbeing.

Aside from the ordinary business of taxation and government spending, the 'ability to pay' principle rightly informs our response to many of the problems we face. When a country suffers a natural disaster, we believe it fitting that people in more fortunate countries should help out – and that the better off a country, the more it should contribute to the relief effort. In the ongoing European migration crisis, there has been a widespread view that it is unfair for the poorer countries of the EU to bear the costs of absorbing refugees simply because they are closer to the frontiers of Europe. Better-off countries to the North of the continent could and should contribute more to alleviating this human tragedy. Climate change is another example. Progress here requires a transition to clean forms of energy production in both rich and poor countries. Justice demands that the poorest of the poor are not required to bear the costs of that transition. So far, richer countries have made many general commitments to fund the rollout of green technology. Making any progress in tackling climate change is going to involve them putting their money where their mouth is.

But global injustice is also an urgent problem. It may not fill our screens as much as natural disasters, migration crises and climate change; but it is at least as deserving of our attention. And here, too, capacity seems to matter. If responding to global injustice is going to involve sacrifices for some, then other things being equal it makes sense to ask more of those who can afford to make more sacrifices.[41] In practice, this need not always mean material sacrifices. In the next chapter we will discuss how individual citizens can best contribute to tackling global injustice. Without pre-empting that discussion, it is at least conceivable that we would do better to devote our efforts to trying to persuade our politicians to take issues of global justice seriously rather than (only) giving up money. If so, our free time and political influence forms an important dimension of our capacity to respond to injustice.

As that example makes clear, however, working out the capacity of different agents can be a tricky process. If the question we face is who ought to admit refugees fleeing from Syria to the frontiers of Europe, capacity to absorb those people will be an important part of the answer. But capacity might be measured in different ways. The idea that richer countries should admit more refugees is certainly plausible. But it might also be argued that we ought to factor in population density, so that countries which were already relatively crowded were asked to admit fewer people. We might also believe it is relevant how the welfare states or healthcare systems in the various European countries are faring, and how they might cope with an influx of vulnerable people. Some people might also believe that we should take account of the culture, religion or language of the receiving countries, on the assumption that the more locals have in common with the refugees in question, the better their integration is likely to go. In some sense what matters fundamentally is how well the various countries are doing, and how well they might fare if they were asked to admit large numbers of migrants. But there is room for disagreement about how best to capture those important facts. Now, the case of global justice is not identical to our hypothetical debate about refugees (as we will see in the next chapter, although admitting more migrants might be one way of advancing global justice, it is one amongst many). But we can expect similar disagreement about the best way to gauge our ability to rectify global injustice.

But however we measure it, capacity surely matters. It may not, however, be the only thing that matters. Taken by itself, the image of the advantaged reaching out to assist the disadvantaged may miss something important. What if the advantaged are, at the same time, complicit in *causing* or sustaining the disadvantage in question? I turn to that idea now.

Contribution to the problem

Often when facing a problem which requires our attention, a key question we will want to ask is: well, who caused it? If we discover that the community centre in our neighbourhood has burned down and needs replacing, it would be odd not to ask questions about who, if anyone, set fire to it. If we eventually find the culprit, it might well make sense to require *them* to pay for a replacement. There may be exceptions to that rule: if the centre was burnt down by mistake, or by a child, that might make a difference. But when people know the likely consequences of their actions, and have alternatives, we tend to think it is appropriate to hold them morally responsible for putting right the wrongs they have done. Such a thought is ever-present in debates about climate change, in which developing countries frequently, and plausibly, argue that those who have knowingly contributed to climate change – by emitting unsafe levels of greenhouse gases – ought to help them deal with its consequences. It could be relevant in migration cases too. If one reason people are fleeing a war-torn country is that another country fuelled its descent into bloodshed, then that second country might have a duty to bear more of the costs of providing refugees with a new home. And it appears just as relevant in the broader case of global justice. Here, then, is a second factor which is relevant to the sharing out of costs: contribution, as well as capability, will often matter.[42]

The trick, in the case of contribution, is to draw the right connection between culprit and consequence. In a complex global economy, doing so is not always going to be easy. As an individual consumer, am I responsible for the tribulations faced by people working in sweatshops on the other side of the world? What if I know little about the existence of sweatshop labour? Might we argue that it is my *duty* to know, if information is readily available? Might someone on the breadline in a developed country argue that he can ill afford *not* to clothe his children in sweatshop clothes, if other options are out of his reach?[43] Any argument which gives a role to causal contribution to global injustice is going to have to deal with complexities such as these.[44] It will also have to clarify which actors are contributors to global injustice. Are injustices caused by states? Or by their individual citizens? Or by their leaders? Or by corporations? Or by the CEOs of those corporations? Or are they sometimes caused by all of these different actors?

Often, the passage of time – and the passing of generations – makes matters still more complicated. If the question is who is responsible for global poverty or inequality, it would be odd not to discuss colonialism and the slave trade. Between the fifteenth and twentieth centuries, Western countries conquered and subjugated much of the rest of the planet. Armed with superior weaponry, our ancestors destroyed communities, pillaged local resources, and contributed to millions of deaths, whether through violence and dispossession or the spread of infectious diseases. Between ten and twelve million people were seized from the continent of Africa so that they could be sold as slaves in the Americas; many of them died miserable deaths on the way. Meanwhile the proceeds of slavery and colonialism bankrolled the construction of ports, roads and canals in the imperial countries, greasing the wheels of their own industrial revolutions. It would be remarkable if slavery and colonialism were not still having an impact on current patterns of prosperity across the world, both for better and for worse. Colonizers, after all, drew often arbitrary lines on maps, creating new 'countries' which are still troubled by conflict centuries later. After destroying or co-opting local elites, they often created institutions which were highly 'extractive' in nature: they focused not on developing the local economy, or including citizens, or sustaining civil society, but on making profits fast, restricting the benefits of development to a lucky few. Indeed, the influence of colonial institutions may still be exerting a drag on progress in the present day.[45]

But when it comes to global justice, the question we need to answer is what *current* generations ought to do, and for whom. And here there are puzzles that we must face. On the one hand, the colonizers have now for the most part left the scene. Whilst current generations may be sitting on the proceeds of slavery and colonialism, they were not complicit in those practices. There might be good arguments why they should contribute to repairing any lasting consequences, but they cannot be based on contribution *per se*. People currently living in rich countries – or so we would hope – may now believe that slavery and colonialism were great wrongs. If we nevertheless believe that descendants should pay the price of slavery and colonialism, perhaps what is doing the work here is simply the idea that these descendants are better off than they would otherwise have been as a result of these injustices, or that they have received advantages which are somehow tainted by their association with colonialism and slavery. On the other hand, we have the question of who any redress is owed *to*. It will not be easy to accurately identify the present-day descendants of slaves, or even of formerly colonized peoples. People move, and countries themselves come and go. Moreover, even if we could identify these descendants, we might not be able to say with any certainty what they are entitled *to*. For that would seem to require us to be able to assess with some confidence how they would be doing if colonialism and slavery had never happened.

And to say this would be difficult would understate matters. None of this, to be clear, is to say that the project of somehow repairing the legacy of colonialism and slavery should be abandoned.[46] But it is to say that the argument must find a way of grappling with some very thorny questions.

When our attention shifts to current generations, however, things become in some respects more straightforward. For we may be able to identify cases where it is relatively clear that actors in the developed world are harming, or setting back the interests of, people in the developing world. For one thing, as we have already noted, the global economy appears to offer distinctly inferior development opportunities to people living in poor countries. Those people often find that their efforts to develop their own way out of poverty are thwarted by the prevailing practices of international trade, whether this means tariffs on food and textiles, the enormous subsidies granted to producers of meat or cotton in rich countries, or the dumping of the unwanted surplus on developing-country markets. On some estimates, the negative consequences of trade practices on people in developing countries easily outweigh the positive impact of overseas aid.[47] Meanwhile, banks and politicians in wealthy countries facilitate the flight of precious capital out of developing countries, for instance by tolerating banking secrecy – ever the friend of the greedy dictator – or by operating tax havens. Again, it has been calculated that potential tax revenues lost by developing countries as a result easily outstrip the foreign aid which flows into the developing world.[48] The international arms trade, too, often makes things worse rather than better in developing countries, allowing dictators to quell or discourage rebellions, and fuelling civil conflict. But it is hugely lucrative, at least for some. The top 100 arms companies have made over $5 trillion selling arms since 2002. Over half of arms exports worldwide come from just two countries – the US and Russia.[49] Many of those weapons flow to countries where we have serious grounds for suspecting they may be used to suppress domestic political opponents.

It is important to recognize here that the rules of international trade are not facts of nature, but are consciously negotiated and chosen by the world's governments. Our leaders could choose differently. It is not inevitable that they should place so much emphasis on the national interest – or, often, the narrow interest of key players in lucrative industries – whether it is by subsidizing domestic producers or tolerating arms exports to brutal regimes. All too often the powerful succeed in shaping the international agenda in their own interest. When they do so, there are costs to the global poor.

Now a reader might wholeheartedly agree at this point, but throw up his or her hands. Certainly the governments of rich countries are unresponsive to the interests of the world's poor. But we often feel they are pretty unresponsive to the concerns of their own citizens too. If a government has been captured by corporate interests, what are the prospects of ordinary citizens changing things? I will return to this issue in the next chapter. For now, though, note that even if the ordinary citizen is powerless to change what his or her government does – which seems unlikely – that doesn't mean that we are not contributors to global injustices. For our everyday acts – including purchases or other consumption decisions – affect the lives of people elsewhere in the world. Some of those acts undoubtedly play a role in making the lives of people in developing countries worse than they would otherwise be.

All too often, in our busy lives, we spare little thought for where the resources that are essential to our lifestyles actually come from. We may be aware of *some* campaigns targeting consumers, certainly. We might be careful, if we are lucky enough to be able to afford diamonds for a loved one, not to buy 'blood diamonds' associated with sustaining civil war in Africa. We might always try to buy 'Fair Trade' coffee or chocolate, because we hope doing so will guarantee a better and more secure livelihood for farmers in Africa and Asia. But the impact of the Fair Trade movement, though often positive, is probably fairly marginal when viewed from the perspective of the global economy as a whole. Meanwhile, many of our purchases put us in a causal chain at the other end of which are dictators or tyrants and the people they oppress. For example, when we fill our cars with petrol, if we engage in any shopping around at all, it's probably driven by price alone. The fact that some petrol supplies might come from dictatorships does not tend to enter our heads. Certainly individual oil companies don't seem to feel the need to market themselves as particularly socially responsible. But these everyday decisions, when aggregated together, can have momentous effects. Our willingness to buy resources sold by dictators, from under the noses of local citizens, can bankroll arms purchases and help corrupt leaders head off pressure for reform.[50] Well-known 'transparency' campaigns – which pressure oil companies to publish information about who they are giving money to, how much, and what happens to it –

are laudable, but so far their effect has again been rather marginal.

We could list countless other ways in which our consumption decisions have significant knock-on effects for poor people around the world. The decision whether or not to eat meat can be enormously consequential. Increased meat production leads to greater competition for land, driving up the prices of the basic foodstuffs which are the staple diet of the world's poor. Our consumption of meat, and also energy, is closely linked with processes of climate change. Doubtless, the precise relationship between any individual act of consumption and an increased probability of cataclysmic climate events is very hard to calculate. But complex changes to the world's climate probably involve many small thresholds, and the chances that our consumption habits over a lifetime may contribute to pushing the climate over one of these thresholds is far from negligible.[51] In other ways, our very wealth appears to make things worse for the world's poor. Rich countries are, compared to developing countries, hugely well served by medical professionals. In the wealthy countries of Europe and North America, there tend to be between 2,000 and 4,000 physicians per million people in the wider population. In Afghanistan, Cambodia and Thailand, the number ranges between 150 and 300. In a country like Tanzania or Ethiopia, the number barely reaches 20.[52] But in developed countries the demand for medical care, often for complaints that would simply go untreated in poor countries, seems to be insatiable. Rather than supporting the healthcare capacity of developing countries, rich countries like the UK frequently free-ride off the resources put into training doctors and nurses in Africa and South Asia by recruiting thousands of them to staff our own – already much more effective – healthcare systems.[53] There have been many proposals for how we might mitigate the losses associated with the medical 'brain drain', but this would require concerted efforts by wealthy countries which they have so far neglected to make.[54]

This raises another key issue when it comes to our causal role in sustaining global poverty or inequality. We are so accustomed to living in a world of nation-states that we rarely pause to consider just what that means for humanity as a whole, and what the alternatives are. Capital, currencies, goods and services flow across national boundaries at incredible speed. But the borders of the nation-state are typically much 'harder' when it comes to people. Although the growth of mass migration has attracted considerable attention, the fact is that entry into wealthy countries is strictly regulated. Admission is by and large the preserve of those with marketable talents, or large sums of money.[55] Most countries have, meanwhile, signed up to international agreements on the rights of refugees which are intended to guarantee protection to people who arrive on our shores after suffering, or being threatened with, per-secution in their home countries. But states have put up a bewildering array of obstacles in order to prevent people claiming asylum from arriving on our shores in the first place, to the extent that legal entry is all but impossible.[56] The consequence of border control techniques, for most people in developing countries, is that it is not possible to improve one's prospects by moving to a place on the earth where conditions are more favourable.

This, too, is not a natural fact but a political choice. As we will see in the next chapter, many economists believe that allowing more immigration from poor countries would be a hugely effective tool of development, with the positive consequences far exceeding those of, say, an increase in aid. There are, as we have just seen, widespread concerns about the impact of the 'brain drain' on developing economies, especially in the healthcare sector. But most economists are confident that the overall beneficial effects of remittances, and the eventual return of workers with new skills, far outweigh the costs.[57] Many people believe, undoubtedly, that their country has a right to control its own borders. Philosophers also continue to disagree about the grounds on which states can exclude outsiders.[58] One view is that we can justly keep borders closed if we agree to assist people in escaping from poverty where they live.[59] For others, the global poor should have the opportunity to escape poverty whether they choose to move or choose to stay.[60] But that is not the point here. The point is simply to recognize that a world of hard borders plays an important role in locking poor people out of opportunities which they could otherwise make use of. Whether we are right to maintain them or not, we should be honest enough to recognize that migration controls are an important mechanism in sustaining poverty and inequality at the global level.

In a whole series of ways, then, we may be making it harder for people to escape poverty, and to enjoy the kinds of prospects which we take for granted in our own lives. At the same time, our countries have signed up to declarations in international law which state that there is a duty on the part of the international community to support the development of poor countries, and especially the very least advantaged.[61] But far from supporting development, much of what we do appears to have the opposite effect. Simply failing to assist those who are much worse off than us represents one kind of global injustice. But so too does making life positively harder for the world's poor.

Recognizing our causal role in sustaining poverty and inequality has important implications for the way in which we should frame debates about global justice. When we portray the contrasting fates of people born into rich and poor countries, one familiar narrative is that of bad luck. People born into the least advantaged countries in our world have been dealt a bad hand compared to people born into the affluent West. Whilst this might work as a metaphor (and I have relied on it myself), it is no more than that. People are not, of course, randomly assigned to countries at the moment of birth. We should be honest enough to recognize that our world assigns membership not on the basis of a roll of the dice, but on the basis of blood and soil – on the basis, that is, of facts about who we are born to, and on which side of the border. More broadly, the narrative of bad luck lets the powerful off the hook too easily. If one reason people in the developing world are poor is that the powerful take decisions that neglect or undermine their own interests, 'bad luck' no longer looks like such a useful term. If the arguments of this section are persuasive, it is more appropriate to see poverty and inequality as the result, to a significant extent, of decisions the powerful make to protect and extend their own privileges.

Tying the strands together

Facts about contribution, as we have just seen, can be very important. One thing they do is reinforce the case for using the language of global *justice*, rather than charity. Imagine that Ellen is deciding whether to give some money to a charity to alleviate poverty overseas, or to take her family out to a restaurant instead. We often think about charitable donations as basically optional. Whilst giving to charity might be the more noble choice in this situation, Ellen is not necessarily *obliged* to make that choice. But this idea – that Ellen is free to choose – would be much less palatable if we knew that she'd helped to *cause* poverty overseas. When we have helped bring about the circumstances in which people lead insecure, degrading or unhealthy lives, the thought that doing something to improve their lot is essentially optional is much harder to defend. If we broke something, we would not be surprised if we were then asked to fix it. Doing so will often be our duty, rather than one option among many we are entitled to take. In the same way, if we have played a role in making the conditions for ordinary people in developing countries worse than they would otherwise have been, it becomes much more plausible that we might have a strict, non-negotiable duty to assist in putting things right. And the greater the role we played, the greater the burden we should carry.

Considerations of contribution, then, can play a significant role when it comes to sharing out the costs of tackling global injustice. As a result, working out which actors are morally responsible for bringing about, or enabling, injustice is a very important endeavour. In cases where we can identify the responsible actors, and other relevant conditions are met – they knew what the consequences of their actions might be, say, and it would have been reasonable to ask them to act otherwise – we appear also to have worked out where the buck for remedying global injustice should stop. Contribution tells us *which* actors to hold responsible for making positive change, and *how much* of the burden of putting things right each of them should bear. Those whose contributions to injustice are more significant should, other things being equal, make greater sacrifices. The CEO at the top of a company responsible for despoiling the local environment in a developing country, or arming its dictator shortly before he went on a killing spree, should probably bear a greater share of the burdens than an ordinary employee who may have known about the wrongdoing, but had less power to stop it.

But whilst contribution is hugely important, we have seen that it is hugely complex too. Cases in which we can neatly identify discrete perpetrators, and tidily delineate the damage they have caused, may be the exception rather than the rule on the global scale. Often as not, we will find ourselves in much murkier waters. To what extent is the underperformance of a developing country's economy down to rigged trade rules, rather than the corrupt mismanagement of the local economy? Just what *is* the lingering effect of slavery? How wealthy would contemporary African countries (many of which did not yet exist as slavery was formally abolished) have been without it? What responsibility do current generations have to remedy the injustices of the past? In many cases teasing out the precise nature of our contribution to global injustice will be difficult and painstaking – but important – work.[62]

In cases where we simply cannot identify contributors – when they have left the scene, or cause and effect are too hard to untangle – we are not morally rudderless, however. In such cases, capacity becomes our moral touchstone. Finding the person responsible for burning down the community centre is a worthwhile endeavour. But when the answer turns out to be that no-one can be held responsible, the centre still needs to be rebuilt. In those cases, it makes sense to allocate burdens in line with our ability to pay. When we allocate costs on the basis of capacity, we ensure that the more difference we can make, the greater the onus there is on us to make an effort. In many cases, the reason why people in the developed world should help those who are faring less well is simply that they can. As we will see in the next chapter, our capacity to make a difference might take a whole variety of forms. It might take the form of moving resources from the rich to the poor, or redrawing many of the global rules which impact on our lives. But one message to hold in mind for now is that the ordinary citizen cannot simply delegate the responsibility to deal with global injustice to his or her political leaders. If you live in a democracy, in which your government is meant to be at least minimally responsive to its citizens, then public campaigns may well make a difference. Global justice is a huge problem, and we all need to do what we can to alleviate it. With the capacity to effect change comes responsibility.

Conclusion

This chapter has examined why issues of global justice are increasingly prominent on the political agenda.

Why Should You Care?

Contemporary debates about global justice reflect an increasing recognition that our fates on a small blue planet are now tied closely together. They also reflect an increasing awareness of our equal moral status, a status which generates significant duties towards people in all four corners of the earth. The struggle for global justice, I have argued, is fundamentally a struggle for a more equal world, as well as one in which severe poverty is consigned to history. That struggle will not be easy, and it will involve people – especially in developed countries – shouldering some costs. I have given an account of how those costs ought to be shared. Needless to say, the struggle for global justice will not be won at one fell swoop. It will be difficult, and there will be setbacks. But there are grounds for hope. In the next chapter, we turn to the means available to those who would fight for a more just world.

3
What Can Be Done?

Progress in a Divided World

Even if you are convinced, by now, that citizens of wealthy countries have a duty to try and alleviate global injustices, what can be *done* about them? Isn't the idea of global justice pie-in-the-sky? Do we really have the power to achieve a better, more equal world? Or are visions of a just world best left to science fiction? And besides, even if progress towards a just world is possible, what can *you*, an individual citizen, do to help?

These questions need to be taken seriously, and not simply wished away. The obstacles in the way of global justice may turn out to be significant. Powerful vested interests stand between us and a more equal world. Meanwhile you – or your fellow citizens – might be sceptical about the prospects for meaningful change. That kind of jaded outlook can become a self-fulfilling prophecy. As we will see, political progress often depends on what we *think* we can achieve, and how we think others are likely to act. As a result, a chance for real change could slip between our fingers without us realizing it.

This chapter aims to tackle pessimism about a better world head-on, and to sow a sense of guarded optimism. It will not attempt to sketch some alternative reality, a utopia in which all injustice has been banished. Instead, it will identify a series of concrete, achievable reforms that would each move us closer to global justice. These reforms are not particularly mysterious, and they are not my own invention either. They build on excellent work done by academics working in politics and economics, by practitioners working for international organizations, and by activists working for charities and non-governmental organizations. In many cases I will be sketching projects which have already begun to have positive effects on the ground, but which need to be pushed further.

Identifying concrete reforms is important, because it is all too easy to condemn the project of global justice as impractical or infeasible. Things are rarely that simple. In the next section we will look a little more closely at what it means to call particular reforms 'feasible' or 'infeasible'. Feasibility, as we will see, is a moving feast, and while there are certainly serious obstacles in the way of greater global justice, this does not mean that significant and worthwhile progress cannot be made. In the section after that, we'll move on to discuss a series of important reforms tackling international trade, tax havens, aid and much else besides. Whilst these reforms do appear to be feasible and important, their success is not a foregone conclusion. They will only come to pass if individual citizens exert pressure on their political leaders. We will finish, therefore, by considering what you or I, as individual citizens, can do to make these reforms more likely.

Is Global Justice Feasible?

Is the idea of global justice wholly impractical? Does it paint a picture of a world we could never reach? Is it, to use a term which has attracted quite a bit of philosophical interest lately, *infeasible*? We might label an achievement as infeasible if it simply cannot be *done*. Some goals, we might think, are infeasible in the sense that they just cannot be brought about. Perhaps asking for a fair or just world is like asking people to move the world closer to the sun, or to reverse the power of gravity. Neither thing is possible. To even try would be a pointless waste of everyone's time.

The first thing to note by way of response is how often we are mistaken about what is feasible and what is not. In the aftermath of the Second World War, the human rights revolution took much of the world by surprise. Today, most of the world's countries have, despite their differences, signed up to a set of core standards describing how they should treat – and refrain from treating – their citizens. Though human rights are frequently abused nonetheless, the agreement that there *are* standards that should be adhered to is a remarkable and in many ways unlikely achievement. For centuries, colonialism – with all of the brutality and exploitation which came along with it – seemed like a fact of political life. Until somehow, between 1947 and 1965, colonial regimes across the planet were toppled. The wave of democratization which swept the world in the 1980s and 1990s, bringing power to millions of ordinary citizens for the first time, was also astonishing to many of the people – including scholars and politicians – who witnessed it.

Within our own countries, we often seem amazingly ready to take for granted the remarkable achievements of the past, and to assume – wrongly – that they were inevitable. In the late 1940s, Britain established a National Health Service amid repeated warnings – including from many doctors – that it was an experiment doomed to failure. Decades later, it is Britain's biggest employer by far, and treats an average of a million people every 36 hours.[1] Even today, many people in the United States firmly believe that to achieve a system of state healthcare, free at the point of use, is an impossibility – or that if it could be achieved, it would be wildly inefficient. Evidence from dozens of countries with free healthcare systems suggests otherwise. But there are many such examples. On the global scale, there has been massive progress in tackling previously intractable diseases such as polio. The world, it seems, is not short of successes which the cynics confidently predicted could not be brought about.

Why are we so often wrong about what is feasible? One reason is that whether something is feasible often partly depends on whether we *think* we can achieve it. If we believe that something is impossible, we may simply not try. And when it comes to politics, things become more complicated still. Here, our views about what is feasible will be partly dependent on what we think *others* will do. If we believe that others will block political progress, we are less likely to make an effort in the first place. If we believe that others will come to our assistance, by contrast, we will be more willing to attempt radical reforms.[2] Rather than dealing with hard and fast facts, our views about what is or is not feasible are bound up with guesses about how other people will tend to act.

The significant point here is that these guesses about how other people are likely to behave are often wrong. At the same time as assuming that past achievements were somehow inevitable rather than surprising developments, we are ready to assume that major changes won't happen in the future, and that things will probably go on much as they have done before. Indeed, we often maintain these beliefs in the face of quite strong evidence to the contrary. Recall the facts about global poverty with which this book began. According to opinion poll evidence, many people believe that it is unrealistic to expect hundreds of millions of people to escape from severe poverty, at least in our own lifetimes. In fact, many people believe that severe poverty is not declining at all, or even that it is getting worse. This flies in the face of the substantial progress made in recent decades, as hundreds of millions of people *have* lifted themselves out of dire need and set themselves on the path to greater prosperity. When we look at the amazing advances which have already been made in tackling poverty, the question becomes not so much *whether* severe poverty can be ended, but *when*. It is not the case, of course, that this progress has been achieved solely – or even mainly – by people consciously aiming to advance the goal of global justice. But nevertheless there is every reason to believe that the reforms I will describe below will make a real difference. Based on current policies, we will probably miss out on the United

Nations' Sustainable Development Goal of eradicating severe poverty by 2030. That failure would be a terrible indictment of a world possessed of such incredible affluence. But it is not a foregone conclusion. It arises, in part, from our failure to take the problem sufficiently seriously – and, perhaps, from an often unjustified pessimism about the prospects of effecting real change. Each of the reforms I will discuss in this chapter would make it much more likely that severe poverty will quickly be consigned to history. Should eradicating severe poverty, then, be ruled out as 'infeasible'? Certainly not. The real question is *when* it will be eradicated, and that depends in part on our political will.

When it comes to inequality, things look much more challenging. Whereas severe poverty has been dramatically declining, rampant inequality remains a stubborn feature of our world. Indeed, the ideal of a world in which everyone enjoys equal prospects in life may well *never* be fully realized. But does this mean we should condemn the goal of global equality for being infeasible? That would be too quick too. Feasibility is not a black-and-white issue. Even in cases where we cannot fully achieve our goals – and success is rarely complete in the messy world of politics – we can satisfy them *to some degree*.[3] We can move *closer* to equality – as well as further away – and even if we never arrive at our final destination, the distance we have covered can be immensely valuable.

This, again, should be familiar from domestic politics. No country has ever achieved perfect equality. But in many places, important victories have been won – including the establishment of welfare states, and free education and healthcare, paid for by progressive taxation. We should not be complacent about those successes – in the 1980s and 1990s, most welfare states were ravaged by cuts; the same has happened again in our more recent era of austerity – but they nevertheless represent major progress towards the goal of ensuring that people's prospects do not depend on their class, race or gender. The vision of a society – or a world – in which people enjoy roughly equal prospects of a good life is not to be ruled out simply because we cannot achieve it at a single stroke – or even by the fact that we may never achieve it at all. Even when progress is slow – even when we seem to be taking two steps back for every one forward – our principles are worth holding onto. The idea of a more equal world can be a guiding light, even when progress is difficult. And, if history is any guide, opportunities can take us by surprise when they do arrive.

Reforms

In 2018, Oxfam reported that the richest forty-two people in the world owned as much wealth as the poorest half of the world's population – or 3.7 billion people.[4] That is a damning indictment of our world. But people sometimes conclude from statistics like these that the solution is simple: we ought to take some of that wealth from the rich, and send it to the poor. Certainly figures like these hammer home that the problem, when it comes to tackling poverty, is not a lack of wealth in the world. There are enormous resources in the global economy, which could potentially be turned to good. But the idea that the solution is just to move money from rich to poor threatens to unduly simplify a more complex picture. For one thing, getting money to the people who need it most may be very difficult – though, as we will see shortly, our capacity to do just that is improving rapidly. Just as importantly, moving money from one place – or person – to another cannot be the whole story. If forty-two people own as much as 3.7 billion, this suggests that something in the global economy is fundamentally broken. The worry is that moving money around – though often helpful – might leave untouched the conditions that allowed massive wealth to arise alongside crushing poverty in the first place – including, not least, the fact that we have an economic system in which real power is wielded by the few rather than the many.

We saw in chapter 1 that disadvantage is not just about a lack of money. Poverty, for example, is also typically characterized by political marginalization and powerlessness. If so, the solution must involve inclusion and empowerment. We should focus on structural changes which would give power to the poor, and put their destiny to a greater extent in their own hands. This is what poor-led social movements in the developing world – such as Slum Dwellers International, the world's largest alliance of groups representing the urban poor, or Via Campesina, a global network of peasant organizations – have themselves emphasized.[5] We have every reason to listen.

This is why, as we will see, the solution to global injustice cannot simply be to increase foreign aid – even if aid is part of the picture. For every dollar of investment or aid the West sends to Africa, still more money flows back *out* of Africa, often in the form of illicit financial flows representing lost tax revenues for African economies.[6] Even if more, and better targeted, aid might be part of the solution to poverty and inequality, we also need to tackle the structural conditions that often lead to money flowing *from* the poor *to* the rich. And this means changing the way in which our economies, and our institutions, work.

What I am not going to offer, though, is a blueprint for what a just world would look like. Would it be a world in which we had transcended capitalism? Almost certainly, if by 'capitalism' we mean a situation in which economic might – and the ownership of productive resources – is concentrated in the hands of a tiny few. That kind of economic inequality all too easily translates into political inequality too, as the rich are able to bend the ears of politicians who come to depend upon them. It is hard to see how justice could be achieved either within societies or between them in the face of such major inequalities. A just world would also be one in which our prospects in life no longer depended upon our sex, or our race, or our religion. Scholars of global justice are slowly coming to pay greater attention to these cross-cutting inequalities.[7] But activists and policy-makers have long understood that enduring change will require putting greater power into the hands of previously oppressed groups – such as women, ethnic and religious minorities, or the disabled. This is why, for instance, the United Nations has made greater gender equality one of its Sustainable Development Goals.[8]

Rather than attempting to describe a fully just world, in what follows, I will sketch seven sets of reforms which would move us closer to that goal. Each can be effective on its own. But they are often mutually reinforcing – and so the more of them we can advance, the better.

But each is, emphatically, a stepping-stone on the road to a more just world, rather than a final destination. Why, though, take this approach at all? Why focus on stepping-stones, when it is the final destination which surely matters? There are at least three reasons. First of all, describing a final destination is all very well, but we need to know how to get there. Identifying specific, achievable reforms which would bring a more just world closer is important in tackling scepticism about the very idea of global justice – in responding, that is, to claims that talk of global justice is infeasible. Second, and relatedly, the problem of global injustice is urgent. This is especially the case when it comes to severe poverty, a problem which ends many lives daily. But burgeoning inequality also demands our attention. In light of the moral urgency of tackling global injustice, I believe it is appropriate to foreground reforms which would have an immediate impact on the lives of ordinary people, even if we dearly hope that more fundamental changes might follow. But this doesn't mean that longer-term or more fundamental changes are kicked into the long grass. To the contrary, many of these reforms would give people in developing countries more power over their own destinies, and as a result make more fundamental change a more realistic prospect. Thirdly, I think it is unwise – and perhaps simply arrogant – for scholars based in the West to presume that they already have a detailed knowledge of what a just world would look like, if only we could get there. Discussions of global justice have, to date, been regrettably dominated by voices from the English-speaking world.[9] Though I have made an effort, in putting together the notes at the end of this book, to draw on work from people from a variety of countries (and from women as well as men), there is no pretending that the conversation on global justice to date has been an inclusive and egalitarian one. That needs to change.[10] But this only shows even more vividly the importance of identifying intermediate steps which would empower people in developing countries to take their own steps on the road to global justice.

In many cases, the reforms we are about to discuss do resonate with the arguments made by activists throughout the developing world. This is important, because it is sometimes suggested that the idea of a more equal world is somehow a Western idea which we impose on the rest of the world at our peril. That idea comes dripping with historical irony. When we have bothered to ask them, the people of the developing world have been clear that they want a fair international order in which they have the genuine chance to catch up with the wealthy countries of the world, rather than being perpetually locked into an inferior position within the global economy. When developing countries gained their independence in the years after the Second World War, their leaders – and citizens – often had very specific ideas about how the international order needed to change in a more egalitarian direction. The first clear visions of global justice – and a new, fairer global economy – arose in the 1970s, and they came not from the imaginations of philosophers and politicians in the West, but from advocates from the developing world.[11] They called for a 'New International Economic Order' which – by offering more aid, more favourable lending, stable prices for commodities, and much else besides – would finally offer poor countries a realistic chance of catching up with the rest.[12] The project ended in disappointment.

But it failed because the leaders of the developed world refused to compromise on their advantages, and not because the developing world did not share with us values of justice, equality and fairness. Although we will no doubt argue over the details in the years to come, the dream of a more equal world is more widely shared than we might think. This is one more reason, as I have suggested, why the reforms discussed below should be seen as the beginning, rather than the end, of the story. The pursuit of global justice must be a partnership, in which ordinary people in the developing world are given 'ownership' of the reforms aimed at improving their life chances, and it must involve sharing power – and ideas – as well as sharing resources.

1. *Trade*

International trade provides one of the most important illustrations of the way in which our fates have come to be bound up together. Patterns of trade have a significant impact on the prosperity of countries across the world. Trade increases the overall productivity of the global economy, by allowing countries to specialize and opening borders to new technology and new ideas. As goods, profits and jobs cross borders with dizzying speed, there have been many winners. China has succeeded in lifting hundreds of millions out of severe poverty – but it is highly unlikely it would have done so without the opportunities offered by trade. Like many other countries in East Asia, it has proven adept at identifying what consumers in wealthy countries want. As Western consumers benefit from more and cheaper consumer products, Asian economies also benefit from exporting them to us.

But it has become apparent that the benefits from international trade are spread very unevenly. The votes for Brexit and for Trump did not come out of nowhere. Among other things, they reflect longstanding discontent about what globalization has done for ordinary citizens, especially in more deprived areas of the UK and the US. Along the so-called 'rustbelt', many voters were ready to march to the beat of Trump's drum: steel workers had lost out to 'unfair' competition from China, and Trump was going to bring the jobs back. For some, this readiness might be puzzling. Economists tell us that trade should bring benefits to all. If some end up losing their jobs to competition from overseas, governments have a ready response: the wealth arising from trade can be used to regenerate areas which lose out, and to retrain people whose jobs have migrated overseas. The populist turn in politics is in part born out of a failure to deliver on this rosy picture. It reflects a widespread – and to some extent justified – belief that the gains from trade have accrued to the haves, rather than to the have-nots.[13]

The gains from trade have also spread themselves very unevenly *between* countries. There have certainly been cases where initially poor countries have gone on to gain a foothold in the global economy. But most trade still flows between a relatively small pool of countries. Aside from East Asian 'tiger economies', the countries which began the twentieth century as the dominant trading powers largely ended it in the very same position.[14] All too often, the role that poor countries find for themselves in the global economy is as exporters of cheap natural resources which will be used elsewhere to manufacture lucrative consumer products. If the poor are ever going to catch up with the rest, something must change.

One reason why poor countries have not made greater gains through trade is that 'free trade' is the official ideology, but much more rarely the practice, of the world economy. Rich countries have brought down many barriers to free trade, by reducing tariffs on imports and harmonizing the regulations which make smooth trade possible. But they have been highly selective in that effort. There has been great progress in opening up trade in high-end consumer products and in services. But these are areas where the rich economies are able to dominate. There has been much less progress in bringing down tariffs in the sectors of the economy – such as food and textiles – where poor countries could genuinely compete if given the chance.

Far from welcoming imports of food or textiles from developing countries, rich countries often protect domestic producers instead. Huge subsidies encourage farmers in Europe and the US to grow more food or cotton than domestic consumers even want. The excess may then be 'dumped' overseas, driving prices down and making life still harder for farmers in the developing world. In recent years social movements in Africa and Asia have protested loudly against such dumping,[15] and there have been a few signs that their protests are being listened to. In 2010 Bill Clinton, the former US President, apologized for the impact that US rice subsidies had had upon the people of Haiti – who, following a devastating earthquake, found themselves desperately in need of food but without the domestic capacity to grow it. Their farmers had long since gone out of business – unable to compete with cheap, subsidized rice imports from the US.[16]

But for the most part, the attention of politicians in wealthy countries has been elsewhere: farmers in rich countries are often concentrated in key constituencies, giving them substantial political influence.[17] The protectionist policies they have argued for make it harder for people in developing countries to escape from poverty. As such they are very hard to justify.[18] Reducing the support offered to farmers – and bringing down barriers to imports from the developing world – could be a painful process. But with appropriate planning and support (including the provision of retraining opportunities), it can be done fairly. The benefits for some of the world's poorest people could be immense. Progress here will mean reducing their dependence on exporting cheap natural resources. Access to markets in food and textiles will be an important intermediate step for many countries. But over time, the goal must be to open up wider opportunities still. The most lucrative markets in the global economy are those in high-end consumer goods and in services. Poor countries should be supported in their tentative steps into those sectors, which look likely to be key to their future prosperity.

Rich countries should undoubtedly open their markets more fully to developing country producers, then. A good example here is the Cotonou Agreement, under which the European Union has agreed to open up its markets to more exports from Africa, Asia and the Caribbean (in return, in many cases, for exporting countries making progress in safeguarding human rights). Such experiments should be extended and deepened. But this does not mean that poor countries should be pressured into opening up their own economies too. For developing countries, pressure to be more 'open' to trade has often meant privatizing public services, and opening domestic industries up to foreign competition before they are ready for it. And in many cases, local governments have very little capacity to assist those who lose out as a result. Instead, poor countries should have greater control over their own economic policies – even if this means that moves towards greater openness are slow and incremental. For some, this solution will sound like hypocrisy: why should rich countries bring down barriers to free trade, if poor countries won't follow suit? The answer is that the freedom to maintain some barriers to free trade appears to be hugely important for the earlier stages of economic development. Countries like the US and the UK themselves maintained 'protectionist' policies (which kept out goods from other countries which would have competed with goods produced domestically) at key stages of their growth. So too did countries like China, Taiwan and South Korea: their moves towards openness in trade were highly piecemeal, and were accompanied by substantial state investment in the economy.[19] There is considerable pressure, from institutions such as the World Bank and IMF, for poor countries to open up their economies as fast as possible. But the success stories of recent years have wisely resisted such advice – just as rich Western nations did before them. International institutions need to learn from what works in different contexts, rather than insisting on a one-size-fits-all policy.

How can such change be achieved? A key role will probably be played by the World Trade Organization. The WTO has often promised to deliver a genuinely pro-poor trade deal for the world. So far, it has failed – not least because rich countries have proven reluctant to make the concessions that would really make a difference to the poor. But stepping away from the WTO is not the solution. With the WTO in deadlock, it has been left to regional free-trade blocs (such as the EU, NAFTA and Mercosur) to make progress for themselves. Bilateral trade deals – between any two countries – have also proliferated. But the least developed countries are often shut out of this process, because they are perceived to have the least to offer. Governments need to re-commit to making progress via the WTO, and ensure that it finally delivers on its stated goal of promoting the development of the poorest. But re-engaging with the WTO will not be enough. Further vital reforms include measures to boost the participation of poor countries in WTO discussions, including subsidized technical assistance. Our representatives at the WTO should also commit to making deals in an open fashion – with the least developed countries in the room – rather than working up deals behind the scenes and presenting them as a *fait accompli*.[20] We need trade fairness, and in order to get it, we are likely to need a fairer decision-making process first.

2. Taxes and transparency

If poor countries are going to develop their economies, then their governments will need funds for investment. But where is the money going to come from? For most countries, the obvious answer is taxation. But herein lies a problem, because developing countries raise much less in tax revenues, as a proportion of GDP, than wealthy countries do. Their capacity to assess what tax is owed, and to collect it effectively, is often quite weak.

For this reason, measures to directly support the ability of developing countries to raise taxes locally are very important. When poor countries rely on foreign aid, their fates are left in the hands of others. Dependence on natural resource exports, meanwhile, leaves poor countries vulnerable to fluctuating prices on world markets, and is often associated with poor governance at home. The more countries are able to support themselves by raising taxes domestically, therefore, the better. These taxes would, of course, have to be calibrated carefully to take account of ability to pay, and avoid pushing the poor deeper into poverty. But in general – though it might sound paradoxical – when states enhance their ability to raise taxes, this bears dividends for citizens too. When governments must rely on citizens to pay their taxes, people tend to have greater control over what their governments do. The more money is taken in tax, the more citizens are typically able to demand by way of effective public services and – crucially – political inclusion. Governments in the developed world can do much to help here. The UK's Department for International Development, for example, has recently worked to support tax-raising efforts in Rwanda and Burundi. By sharing technical expertise, a partnership for development has been built which has already paid major dividends.[21]

These measures can achieve a good deal, and in many cases they already have. But there is another side to the picture. Regrettably, the wealthy world has done much to *undermine* the ability of poor countries to stand on their own two feet financially. The reality is that there is a major flight of wealth out of poor countries, and towards wealthier ones. The effect is to starve local economies of much-needed resources. In many cases, this flight takes an illicit form – as when the proceeds of crime, money-laundering and tax evasion are spirited away into foreign bank accounts. The sums involved are staggering. Between 2004 and 2013, the developing world lost $7.8 trillion in illicit financial outflows.[22] Illicit flows of wealth *from* developing countries outweigh total *incoming* investment from the rest of the world – even when we include development aid. For each dollar that flows into many poor countries, two or three flow out again. And these illicit flows are growing, rather than shrinking.

The problem has many sources. One of them is aggressive tax avoidance on the part of multinational corporations operating in the developing world. Dubious accounting mechanisms allow countries making profits in developing countries to base themselves for tax purposes in countries where tax rates are much lower.[23] 'Tax havens' will happily offer on-paper homes to corporations, even if the goods and services from which they profit are produced and consumed elsewhere. The publication of the Panama Papers (in 2016) and the Paradise Papers (in 2017) brought home to the wider public the enormous scale of tax avoidance and tax evasion practised by companies, rich individuals and even some politicians. If outsiders are complicit in sustaining this flight of capital, we may be doing more harm than good in the developing world. But remedies are available. Here I will highlight three key reforms which would empower poor countries to deal with the problem.

The first is greater global sharing of data about the source and ownership of financial assets – culminating, ideally, in a global financial register recording ownership of financial assets worldwide. Public sharing of information on global income and wealth could be an important prelude to more ambitious reforms, such as global wealth taxes or income taxes.[24] In the meantime, it would allow developing countries – and rich countries too – to ensure that the winners in the global economy pay their dues. The technology to track money across borders is already within our reach. Recent measures to tackle money-laundering and the financing of terrorism have shown that, when the political will exists, that capacity can be put to good use. The challenge is to make the sharing of knowledge about financial flows the norm rather than the exception. Ninety-six countries have already committed to key international standards on the automatic exchange of financial information. Those countries which have lagged behind should be pressured to come on board. Some of the least developed countries, meanwhile, may need technical support to participate in the process.[25]

A second goal is a much greater degree of international tax coordination. At present, many countries compete to play host to wealthy corporations. And they do so by maintaining low rates of corporate taxation. Countries which want to maintain better public services – and pay for it via higher rates of taxation – will often see corporations relocating to low-taxing states. This competition has only one set of winners: the corporations which can shift their operations – at least in name – to tax havens. But it has many losers – including ordinary citizens in both rich and poor countries. But countries can and should fight back, by cracking down on tax havens and agreeing to maintain reasonable and consistent levels of taxation.[26] Such a proposal is not pie-in-the-sky. It does not require the establishment of new global institutions. It simply requires countries to cooperate to present a more united front to the world's wealthy corporations. Developing countries could be major winners from such coordination. But wealthy countries can gain too. More than a tenth of global wealth is now held in (often secret) tax havens. Roughly a fifth of the corporate profits made in the United States are 'booked' in tax havens, rather than being available to fund public services in the US.[27]

Third, let us return to the powerful theme of transparency. Transparency can help poor countries to tackle the flow of money out of their borders. But transparency about flows of money *into* poor countries can also empower ordinary citizens. As we noted earlier, many developing countries have found for themselves an unenviable niche in the global economy, as exporters of the natural resources – including, most prominently, oil – on which our economies depend. But the resulting revenues are all too easily captured by unscrupulous leaders. Far from making things better in developing countries, these revenues often serve only to protect dictators from popular demands for reform.[28] Citizens can hardly demand that rulers spend resource revenues on decent public services if they do not know who is paying how much to whom. In such a context, simply requiring corporations based in the West to 'publish what they pay' can be a powerful agent for change.[29] More broadly, rulers in resource-rich developing countries can be encouraged to place resource revenues in trust for the wider population. Many countries (including Kuwait, China and Malaysia) already channel revenues into 'Sovereign Wealth Funds' capable of funding major development projects, now and in the future. The important thing is that these funds are democratically and transparently run, and that they have a clear brief to work to eradicate poverty.[30] Countries which have succeeded in doing that should share their experiences with countries which are newer to the resource trade.

If we can achieve these reforms, they will increase the power of people in developing countries to improve their own societies. They will empower local governments. And the more ordinary citizens are involved, the better.

3. Lending and investment

Increasing the capacity of poor countries to raise tax revenues is important, but it may not be enough. It will take time for tax revenues in poor countries to approach anything like the levels seen in the West. In the meantime, funds for investment in infrastructure, education and other public services are badly needed.

Unfortunately, poor countries' access to capital from abroad is largely unfavourable. The lending available to poor countries is expensive, and often comes with strings attached.[31] The World Bank and the IMF officially aim to promote growth, and especially pro-poor growth, by lending to countries which are experiencing difficulties. But they have a chequered history.[32] In return for loans, they have often insisted on free market reforms, including opening up borders to the free movement of capital. In theory this should help poor countries in need of private investment from abroad. In practice, it has often simply made it easier for still more wealth to flow outwards. The removal of restrictions on capital flows has had very mixed results,[33] and – especially in Africa – it appears to have increased inequality.[34]

Critics of the World Bank and IMF would also point out that the 'reforms' these lenders have favoured have stripped back state provision of education and healthcare, and worsened the human rights records of developing countries.[35] They have, moreover, encouraged poor countries to sign deals to sell local natural resources on highly unfavourable terms.[36] But probably the biggest complaint against the policies of the IMF and World Bank is that they simply have not *worked* to promote pro-poor growth (though they have opened up lucrative opportunities for companies moving into newly privatized sectors). Countries which comply with IMF recommendations seem to grow slower, rather than quicker, than other countries. The strings attached to loans, meanwhile, tie the hands of governments, making them less responsive to the needs and views of local citizens. They have served to place considerable power into the hands of a class of international bureaucrats with a limited record of success. Successful development policy will pay heed to local realities, rather than adopting a one-size-fits-all approach.[37] The World Bank and the IMF have shown signs of recognizing this, but progress has been too slow.

Against this background, poor countries have often, unsurprisingly, turned away from the IMF and World Bank, and sought funds from other sources instead. China (and to a lesser extent India) has ploughed billions into infrastructure projects in Africa in return for a stake in its natural resource wealth.[38] The results have been mixed but probably no worse, on balance, than the record sheet of the IMF and World Bank. But perhaps the latter institutions are not beyond reform. Rather than being consigned to irrelevance, both of them should adopt a still more flexible approach, especially when it comes to their insistence on privatization and the removal of capital controls. And both should promote much greater developing country involvement throughout the development process. At present, a small number of wealthy countries – and particularly the US – exert a disproportionate influence on decision-making in both institutions. For voting power to track wealth in this way is not compatible with viewing people from rich and poor countries as moral equals.[39] At every stage – from policy-making to the evaluation of results – we should expect the full participation of leaders and ordinary citizens from the developing world.

Two final reforms also deserve our attention. The first involves assistance for developing countries struggling to service debts racked up in the past. In general, we believe that people ought to repay their debts. But what if the debts in question are 'odious' – what if, that is, they were borrowed, and often squandered, by unaccountable rulers who have now left the scene? Ordinary citizens may never have been consulted in this process, and may never have seen any of the benefits.[40] Paying back these loans, however, can make progress in advancing even the most basic rights of citizens that much harder.[41] In such a scenario, a good case can be made for writing off historical debts. There has already been some progress in this direction. But once again, there are typically strings attached: the recipients of debt relief must agree to enact free-market reforms which have at best an unproven record, and which at worst could make things still worse for the poorest of the poor. If debt relief is to be conditional at all, it should be conditional on actual progress in tackling poverty and exclusion, and not on the uptake of particular free-market policies favoured by international lenders.

A second reform concerns the world of private investment. As well as loans from international lenders like the World Bank, the poorest countries are often desperate to attract investment from foreign corporations. But overseas investors have often asked for an extraordinary degree of protection for their investments – and received it. Now, the idea that when corporations choose to invest their money in developing countries they should have their interests protected is not entirely unreasonable. If local countries could simply confiscate corporations' property, say, there would not be much of an incentive for them to invest in the first place. But the full extent of the assurances poor countries have been asked to give overseas investors is remarkable. According to so-called 'stabilization clauses' written into many investment treaties, companies which invest in developed countries are entitled to sue local governments whenever any changes in the law mean that their anticipated profits are affected. In practice, this means that governments wishing to beef up environmental protections, or bolster health and safety laws affecting local workers, or raise corporate taxes, find themselves liable for massive claims for compensation. Companies have proven highly aggressive in pursuing such claims. Local governments face the threat of expensive arbitration and a potentially massive bill for compensation at the end of the process. Unsurprisingly, they often simply decide to cave in to corporate demands, rolling back any proposed changes in the law before they take effect.

This little-known 'investor-state dispute settlement system', in sum, has a seriously chilling effect on developing countries' ability to introduce progressive regulation of labour and environmental standards.[42] The system is in urgent need of reform.[43] The secretive world of tribunals should be opened up to public scrutiny, and companies which seek to prevent progressive legislation in the developing world should be named and shamed. More broadly, Western countries should agree not to enforce clauses in investment treaties which grant such a remarkable degree of protection to multinational corporations. For shareholder interests to trump the rights of the world's poor in this way is unacceptable.

4. Aid

When it comes to the struggle against poverty and inequality, few topics are as controversial as foreign aid. Its supporters have made great claims about the potential for scaling up foreign aid and ending poverty.[44] Most rich countries have committed themselves to giving 0.7 per cent of their GDP in the form of overseas aid. Though very few of them have met it, this target might allow us to make substantial progress in consigning poverty to history. Enter the sceptics, who claim that much aid money is wasted, that it feeds a bloated aid industry as well as corrupt governments, and that it may even make things worse for the world's poor.[45]

The devil, unsurprisingly, is in the detail. Aid has often failed to promote economic growth. But it has not always *aimed* to do so – at least not directly. Much aid aims to reduce disease or infant mortality, for example – noble efforts even if they do not show up immediately in the economic accounts. Less honourably, aid has frequently been an instrument of foreign policy, securing the cooperation of the allies of the West – whether in the fight against communism or, more recently, Islamic terrorism. For aid to fail to tackle poverty in such circumstances is hardly a surprise. It is important to recognize, though, that aid *can* work.[46] It has helped eradicate smallpox, and assisted the fight against AIDS, for instance. Even its critics accept that, in the case of support for vaccination and other health programmes, aid has saved millions of lives.[47] To a significant extent, then, the debate should not be so much about whether the sheer amount of aid should be more or less than it is now. The challenge is to take on board the many lessons about when aid works, and when it does not. Even if much aid is wasted, we can learn a considerable amount from the cases where it does good. In *those* cases there will often be scope for increasing our contributions. We need better aid, and not merely more of it.

Some of the lessons of aid practice should not, in fact, be difficult to learn. For one thing, aid is often unreliable. A surprising proportion of what is promised simply fails to materialize.[48] The unpredictability of aid only makes things harder for poor countries which may already struggle in the face of fluctuating prices for the commodities they are able to sell. Aid flows should be something which recipients can count on in advance, unless there are clear grounds for suspecting that it is doing more harm than good in a particular case. A second problem is that aid is often uncoordinated. Recipient states have to contend with the demands of multiple donors, each of whom might want to attach different strings to their funding. Donors ought to sing from the same hymn sheet, and stick to a clear set of benchmarks for success, which give recipient communities a degree of autonomy over how they are to be achieved. Since the Paris Declaration on Aid Effectiveness in 2005, there has been some progress in this direction, but not yet enough. One kind of 'string' which is often attached to aid ought to be cut entirely. The 'tying' of aid requires recipients to spend aid money exclusively on goods or services from the donor country (the US has been particularly fond of this practice). But whilst it is often good for Western companies, this offers bad value for poor countries. It also means that official figures on aid are inflated: much of the money quoted in figures on US aid, for instance, never actually leaves the US. Finally, aid is often poorly targeted (not least when it goes to our allies rather than those who need it most). There is evidence that, in the post-Cold War period, the targeting of aid to the needy has improved.[49] But there is still a long way to go. On some estimates, aid could achieve twice as much good if we were simply more consistent in channelling it to the poorest.[50] Meanwhile Britain's Department for International Development has been threatening to move in the other direction: in the post-Brexit world, it is said, aid should be used to promote trading relationships with the UK. Fortunately, the majority of the British public disagree: aid should be directed on the basis of need, not our own national interest.[51]

In finding the way forward, donors should also pay close attention to some innovative recent experiments in aid delivery. Often, so-called sceptics about aid turn out to be sceptics about a particular *kind* of aid: money sent from one government to another.[52] The fear here is that even if the intentions of donors are good, aid money can end up being spent for the wrong purposes, and might end up bolstering the position of unrepresentative rulers. But there are other ways of giving aid. A new wave of international aid policy has emphasized the importance of more accurately – and independently – assessing the effectiveness of giving.[53] One promising example involves giving cash directly to poor families in some of the world's least advantaged countries. Mobile phone technology now means that payments can be made even to people without bank accounts. The organization GiveDirectly, for instance, sends no-strings cash grants straight to poor families in Kenya and Uganda.[54] Despite fears that this money would be squandered or that it would fuel inflation, the results have generally been impressive. Independent assessments have judged these experiments to be effective at reducing child labour and increasing school enrolment, improving health outcomes, and reducing early marriage and pregnancy.[55] Direct transfers of cash may not be a magic bullet when it comes to ending poverty; much else needs to change too. But direct cash transfers can help us to avoid some of the problems which can accompany aid. Far from bolstering the power of rulers, direct transfers put power straight into the hands of citizens in developing countries, opening up an array of new opportunities.

When it comes to securing global justice, aid is likely to be part of the picture for some time to come. In the case of humanitarian emergencies, aid is a vital part of the response. When it comes to the more everyday matter of promoting development, it is not going to be the whole story by any means. But it can be an important tool, and if well targeted it can be very effective. It can help poor countries deal with a shortage of capital; and it can make important reforms more likely, by easing the costs to domestic constituencies.[56] Given its potential, it is hugely important that donors learn the lessons of past decades about when aid works and when it fails. In many cases, this will mean giving more of a voice to local people, making aid less of a top-down process and more of a partnership for development, in which aid is predictable and local people are involved in setting priorities. Increasingly – although, again, there is no one-size-fits-all solution – successful aid will also involve putting resources in the hands of individual citizens, so as to give them greater power over their own destinies.

5. Migration

A number of economists have recently argued that, if we are wondering how the wealthy world can help promote the development of the poorest countries, we should be paying much greater attention to migration.[57] Migration from the developing to the developed world is good for migrants themselves, giving them access to higher wages and a wider set of opportunities. But it has wider positive effects. Migrants send back money – so-called 'remittances' – to loved ones; and they often return eventually to their countries of origin, bringing along with them new skills, ideas and networks.

Within political discussion, the positive effects of migration for poor countries are often drowned out by concerns about the 'brain drain' – and particularly what happens when wealthy societies recruit healthcare workers from countries with crumbling healthcare systems. But this worry may make things too easy for us. Overall, emigration is often beneficial for 'sending' countries. Even the *chance* to emigrate can encourage people to develop lucrative skills. Perhaps for this reason, African countries with the greatest outflows of doctors and nurses, somewhat surprisingly, have better health out-comes than those with lower outflows.[58] To this we can add the effects of remittances, and the sharing of ideas and networks. On balance, the positive effects of migration on poverty are already considerable – and this is in a world of relatively closed borders.[59]

For some scholars, in fact, migration looks like the *most* effective means we currently have of promoting development abroad. One way of tackling global injustice, then, would be for rich countries to accept more migrants from the developing world. This would not require them to build new institutions, or to secure international agreement. Each country could simply choose to welcome more people from the developing world. If they did, the effects could be dramatic. Remittances sent to Africa are *already* greater than foreign aid, and they typically flow directly to individuals, rather than being routed through often unaccountable governments.[60] In the past they have cushioned poor societies against the impact of rising food prices,[61] and provided much-needed funds for investment. There is surely scope, we might think, for migration to do still more good. The fruits of such a policy would be still greater if wealthy countries admitted relatively low-skilled migrants (who have the most to gain from migration), rather than cherry-picking those with lucrative – and scarce – skills.

But is a greater openness to migrants politically likely? Rich countries are home to rapidly ageing populations, and birth rates continue to fall. At some point they will need to admit significant numbers of workers from abroad if they are to sustain healthy economies. But immigration is a political hand-grenade. A feeling that the borders have been *too* open undoubtedly played some role in the votes for Brexit and for Trump. What scope, then, for making our borders more open still? The problem we face is rather similar to that posed by international trade. Trade and migration *do* bring net benefits for rich countries. But it is not enough to simply wait for the benefits to trickle down to the working classes. The local consequences of migration must be managed properly. This, unfortunately, is not what has happened. Instead, successive governments have failed to cushion local communities from the impact of increased demands on public services. Meanwhile public attitudes to immigration are, if anything, hardening.[62]

One suggestion here is that we could sweeten the political pill by making migration a better deal for receiving countries. We could admit more migrants, but give them an inferior set of rights to health and social services, or restrict their employment opportunities compared to local workers. Moving would still be worthwhile for the migrant, but it would become more lucrative for rich countries. Such a deal might make migration more politically acceptable.[63] But we should be wary of such compromises. Enhancing the opportunities available to the global poor matters. But so too does the ideal of social equality – and this is incompatible with a society where some people are permanently condemned to a second-class status. But in any case, the political failure to manage migration successfully is not inevitable. The correct response is not to turn away from migration, any more than it is to turn away from trade. Such a reaction would make the global poor pay the price of our own political failures – and our prejudices. We should pay closer attention to the various different interests at stake here – balancing the needs of employers and the working classes in receiving countries, and low- and high-skilled migrants from sending countries. Above all, we should continue to make the positive case for the benefits of migration – for the rich and the poor – *and* fight, at the same time, to make sure that the impact of migration is properly managed at the local level.

6. The arms trade

Poor governance – including, at the extreme, brutal dictatorship – has slowed progress towards tackling poverty and exclusion in many developing countries. Dictatorship is a curse from the point of view of local citizens. But the actions of outsiders often make the emergence, or survival, of dictatorships more likely. One of the most direct examples is the global arms trade. Dictators require weapons to gain, and keep, their hold on power. But relatively few countries manufacture arms in significant quantities. For the most part, dictators are able to find ready supplies of weapons from overseas.

The market for arms is a highly lucrative one. Ninety per cent of the world's weapons are manufactured in just ten countries.[64] The United States is the largest exporter, with roughly a third of the global market.[65] Whilst it has a number of regulations controlling the arms trade, arms continue to be diverted to conflict-torn countries. Since the 9/11 attacks, the US has dramatically increased sales to oppressive regimes, including many countries which its own State Department has criticized for human rights abuses.[66]

It is not obvious that arms sales to dictators are always unjustified. Sometimes dictators are struggling to maintain power against rebels whose rule would be still worse for local people.[67] But too often arms sales are driven by commercial interests at the expense of humanitarian considerations. In 2014 a major international Arms Trade Treaty came into effect, which aimed to bring some core standards to the industry. Though it is too early to judge its full impact, activists are concerned that it contains too many loopholes. It declares that manufacturers should not sell weapons in cases where they know they will be used for illegitimate ends – such as repressing civilians. But this sets the bar too low. Arms are often sold to (relatively) legitimate buyers, and then quickly sold on to those who are less scrupulous about human rights. Sales should also be prohibited when experience suggests there is a substantial risk that they are going to be diverted.[68]

Other key reforms would include intensified vetting earlier in the process of arranging arms sales. By the time contracts are in the offing, governments find it hard to ignore the lobbying of major arms companies, which will caution that job losses are likely if deals are not fulfilled. Greater transparency earlier in the process can help here. The arms business is, unsurprisingly, a secretive one. But concerted action by activists and concerned citizens can be effective in preventing illegitimate sales at the outset. Countries should also be prevented from hiding behind blurred legal lines. Weapons sold for policing – an apparently legitimate activity – are often used to repress those who dare to protest against unaccountable leaders. This too ought to be prevented. In general, the problem of controlling the arms trade ought to be mainstreamed into discussions about development.[69] If not, the good work which can be done by trade or aid can be undone through the back door. To give aid for development on the one hand, and enhance the ability of oppressive governments to hold off pressure for reform, on the other, makes no moral sense.

7. Climate change

Climate change threatens serious consequences for many of the world's worst-off people. Though sea-level rises and unpredictable weather patterns will undoubtedly affect people living in rich countries too, they will hit the poor hardest. Left unchecked, climate change may mean that millions of people lose their livelihoods and their homes.

This urgent problem generates several priorities. The first is to get serious about the mitigation effort. The world must wean itself off reliance on fossil fuels for most of its energy, and fast. But the burden of the transition to green energy must not – and cannot – be borne by the poor. At the same time as making changes to their own lifestyles, the privileged must share their technology with developing countries. It is in no-one's interest for development in poor countries to be as dirty as our own has been. But neither is it fair to require the world's poor to hold back on their struggle against poverty. The United Nations has already established proven mechanisms for channelling funds and technology towards developing countries seeking to make the transition to clean energy. The Green Climate Fund is the most prominent example.[70] But it is seriously underfunded: its goal of raising (and spending) $100 billion per year is nowhere near being met. Despite having pledged $3 billion, for example, the US has transferred just $1 billion to date. The vague promises of our politicians must be converted into hard cash. As well as funding the spread of green technologies into the developing world, attention must also be paid to the plight of poor countries which currently export fossil fuels. When we ask such countries to 'leave the oil in the soil', they may well respond that they have few other opportunities for growth. If the cost of mitigating climate change is not to fall on the shoulders of the poor, this demands that we help open up other development paths.[71] Here too the Green Climate Fund could make an important contribution.

Funds should also be targeted at preventing another major source of climate change: deforestation. It might seem perverse to give money to countries which agree to protect their rainforests. The scenario sounds a little like hostage-taking: give us the money, a forest community might say, or the forest gets it. But payments for protection are both morally defensible and politically urgent. Given the vital roles that rainforests play on our planet, we have a collective interest in their preservation. Right now, the costs of their protection – including development opportunities which are lost when land can't be used for other purposes – fall on low- (and some middle-) income countries across the world's tropical regions. This is unfair.[72] Payments to countries which make demonstrable progress in arresting illegal deforestation can ease the tragic choice between poverty and conservation. Likewise, so-called 'debt-for-nature' swaps – which tie the cancellation of debt to the preservation of the forests – also have some promise.[73]

Even if these policies work, however, some degree of climate change is already with us. Because of their role in causing climate change, and because of their greater ability to make sacrifices, the developed world owes it to the world's poor to help them to adapt to the changes it brings, and to assist them to find new livelihoods – and even new places to live – when they cannot. Climate change is a complex problem which will require a multi-pronged response.

What Can *I* Do?

In the last section, I described a series of reforms which would make a real difference when it comes to tackling global poverty and inequality. All of these reforms will require global partnership: the project of global justice cannot be reduced to 'us' driving through changes to make 'them' better off. In many cases they will involve empowering local communities, and giving them a greater voice in international forums. But at the same time there is an important role for concerned citizens in the developed world to play. Even if we do not have all of the answers, we enjoy privileges and influence that many people in the developing world can only dream of. And with that power comes responsibility.

But what can you, as an ordinary citizen, do to make the reforms sketched above more likely to come about? People often become switched off from politics precisely because they find it hard to believe that they *can* make a real difference. Political scientists, in fact, sometimes tell us that it is a wonder that anyone participates in politics at all. One vote among millions, after all, is highly unlikely to be crucial to any given outcome. In the same way, adding one solitary voice to the argument for greater global justice may seem like a mere drop in the ocean.

But it's important not to give in to that kind of fatalism. Change does happen, and the major changes of the past have had small beginnings. In this section I will describe some of the ways in which you can make a difference, and give some hints as to how to make your interventions more, rather than less, likely to be effective. Part of the message here is that we already *do* have an impact on the lives of others – as voters, as consumers, as activists and in many other ways besides. The question is not, therefore, *whether* our actions are going to influence people's life chances across the planet. The question is *how*. I've suggested in this chapter and the last that in some cases, our actions actually appear to make things harder for people living in the developing world. Can we avoid some of these negative effects – and even do some good for people in the developing world?

Be a smart consumer
Unless we opt for a self-sufficient life, we cannot help but be consumers. And it is in our role as consumers that we make some of our most direct impacts on the wider world. By educating ourselves and by making responsible choices, we can make a difference. Sometimes this will mean choosing to consume *less*. And sometimes it will mean choosing to consume *differently*.

Our world faces major environmental problems – from increasing pressure on scarce resources, to the damaging consequences of climate change and plastic pollution. Thinking about our consumption of energy and plastics, for instance, or taking seriously the impact of our travel habits, can open up ways forward. Until renewable technologies come online on a sufficient scale, actions to reduce our energy consumption will be at a premium. When it comes to travel, buying a hybrid or electric car – if you can afford one – will reduce your carbon footprint considerably. So will cutting down on air travel, or 'offsetting' your carbon consumption if you do fly. For those lucky enough to have the option, working from home one or two days a week can generate a considerable carbon saving. You may have access to subsidies aimed at improving your home's insulation, or making solar panels more affordable. Switching energy supplier to one which draws on renewable sources can also make a big impact. Finally, cutting down on your consumption of meat can advance several goals at once: doing so reduces your carbon footprint, lessens pressure on fragile water sources, and eases competition for land (which often serves to drive up food prices, including for the global poor). There are numerous options for reducing your ecological 'footprint', and many of them can be cost-effective for the individual consumer too.

Decisions about *which* goods to buy can also be very consequential. The 'Fair Trade' movement, for instance, will already be familiar to most. Fair Trade goods are not a cure-all for global injustice by any means: so far, the impact of the Fair Trade movement has probably been quite modest.[74] But progress has been made in guaranteeing producers in poor countries a sustainable living wage. At the same time, the market for Fair Trade goods sends out a wider signal that consumers care about more than just the bottom line – and that other producers ought to take seriously labour and environmental standards, workers' rights and the importance of sustainable livelihoods.

Consumers can and do use their purchasing power to encourage good corporate conduct, and to deter exploitative or environmentally destructive practices. Boycotts can be an effective tool of 'informal' consumer action, especially when the institutional capacity to punish those who commit wrongs is weak.[75] To be effective, boycotts should be organized. If one individual stops buying a particular good, the effects may be negligible. But taken *en masse*, our actions can exert real pressure. Boycotts should therefore be accompanied by a fanfare of publicity aimed at encouraging others to join with us. They should also be carefully targeted. Simply refusing to buy from a particular business may achieve little. For boycotts to be effective, they should make specific and *achievable* demands. If the targets are selected carefully, other businesses can be encouraged to put their own houses in order too.[76] One obvious goal for consumer campaigns would be greater transparency on the part of multinational corporations. Companies should be encouraged to publish clear figures on what they pay to governments in the developing world, and what they demand in return. While the results have not been perfect, the 'blood diamonds' campaign emanated in the Kimberley Process for certifying conflict-free diamonds, and has succeeded in reducing the human rights abuses often associated with the industry.[77] The argument for extending the approach to other industries seems clear. Another good target for consumer pressure would be companies which resort to the threat of international arbitration to dissuade developing world governments from legislating to protect workers or the environment.

Consumer campaigns should not be limited, however, to the food, clothes or jewels that we buy. We are also enmeshed in webs of influence – and, sometimes, harm – in our capacity as investors. You may not, of course, be used to thinking of yourself as an investor.

But if you have a pension or a bank account, your savings will indeed be invested somewhere. In recent years 'divestment' campaigns – which seek to persuade fund managers to shift their investments out of ethically dubious industries – have gained a higher and higher profile. One famous example is the movement for fossil fuel divestment. If we are to avoid dangerous climate change, most fossil fuels will have to be left in the ground. But if so, those whose pensions depend on the performance of oil and gas companies are in for a rude awakening.[78] Here prudence as well as morality may dictate that we take our money out of the fossil fuel industry. At the same time, we should be clear about what we expect the practical effects of divestment campaigns to be. If we sell our shares in ethically dubious industries and others simply step in to buy them instead, little will have been achieved. Still, divestment will send a clear signal that we consider some industries to be harmful – and that they are not the kind of industries that governments ought to be supporting with large tax breaks and subsidies.[79] Similarly, if your bank invests in the arms trade, or in companies associated with exploitative practices in the developing world, you might consider switching to an ethical alternative. But if you do, tell them about it. Even better, tell them that you're going to tell others about it too. When it affects a company's bottom line, reputation matters.

Give

Achieving a more just world will involve structural change which hands power back to people in the developing world, opening up for them the kinds of opportunities which we have learned to take for granted. But achieving structural change requires us to build coalitions for reform, and can take a good deal of time and patience. Moreover, the path to meaningful reform is often paved with frustration. In the meantime, however, we can still have a direct positive impact on the lives of people living in very unfavourable conditions around the world. One way in which to do this is to give money to a reputable development charity. There have been high-profile arguments for people to give a fixed proportion of their income – such as 5 per cent or 10 per cent – to charity.[80] Certainly, donations on that scale can have a significant effect: on one calculation, an average earner in the US, sacrificing 10 per cent of their income, could pay for in the region of 44,000 mosquito nets during their lifetime.[81] But even much smaller donations can make a real difference. Giving is something an individual can do at any time, to the degree that they feel able.

The general public are often rather sceptical about the difference that our donations can make in practice.[82] We ought to be careful about giving too easy a rein to that scepticism, because it promises to make things very easy for us. The jaded claim that nothing will ever change is a common cover story for the refusal to share our advantages with others. Fortunately, enormous progress has been made in recent years in the independent assessment of the effectiveness of charitable donations. Organizations like GiveWell[83] and Charity Navigator in the US[84] deliver accessible information about how you can have the maximum impact when you give. They can help to identify the most effective charities to which you could donate.[85] At present, their recommendations focus on restoring eyesight, funding research into neglected tropical diseases, and protecting people against malaria and parasitic worms. Each pound, or dollar, given to a charity working in those fields can help improve the lives of individuals afflicted by life-threatening or life-changing conditions which, in the West, would be treated as a matter of course. These charities also tackle another common complaint against aid charities by providing information on the most efficient charities, in which the highest proportion of your donation finds its way to the poor people who can benefit from it.

As of 2018, GiveDirectly was also one of the top-rated charities according to GiveWell. According to its independent analysis, GiveDirectly deserved praise for its high degree of transparency, and its strong track record in making sure that donations are targeted appropriately at families which can benefit from them.[86] To repeat a theme from above, aid is far from the only thing that matters when it comes to advancing global justice. It is not an alternative to deeper reform. But it can and does achieve results, and we are learning a good deal more, as time goes by, about what makes interventions more or less successful. In a context of widespread cynicism about the prospects for a fairer world, it is worth making the case that the ability to make a positive difference to individual lives in the developing world is often much closer at hand than we think.

Engage, campaign and organize
Though we can make a difference as individuals – whether by giving, or being intelligent and responsible in our decisions as consumers – we can achieve much more together than we can apart. Many of the great political changes of past generations have come to pass following extensive organization and coalition building.

What Can Be Done?

An individual citizen could be forgiven for despairing about global injustice if he or she tried to tackle the problem alone. But it isn't necessary to struggle alone. One of the reasons we have political institutions in the first place is that they allow us to accomplish more through working together than we could achieve individually. At the same time, they reduce the burdens on any particular individual, ensuring that we do not have to devote our every waking hour to the task of making the world a better place.[87] The same goes for less formal political coalitions, which express and demonstrate the combined political power of their supporters. In order to be successful, these coalitions for global justice must ultimately bring together both the citizens of wealthy democracies and citizens of developing countries.

Many of the reforms we have discussed in this chapter require political will. The reforms I have described do not require us to create new institutions at the global level; but they do require our politicians to do the right thing. And, judging from history, there is no guarantee that they will do that. But, living in (more or less imperfect) democracies, we do have critical levers available to us. Politicians need to be re-elected. If enough of a politician's constituents care about an issue, then he or she needs to care about it too, and fast.

In the contemporary world we have a number of means of communicating our priorities and our values, from the traditional to the innovative. Manifestos and party websites provide information about the policies of the various political parties. On the web, it is easy to find out the contact details of our representatives. Letters to their constituency offices will be read, and usually answered (though there is no guarantee that you will like the answer). Members of parliament can also be emailed directly. But again, an individual letter or email is precisely that: a hand held out by a solitary individual. Our messages come to be genuinely effective when they resonate with other messages being received by our politicians. Online petition sites like Avaaz have succeeded in mobilizing hundreds of thousands, and sometimes millions, of concerned citizens. In those numbers, politicians are obliged to take serious notice. As Avaaz's website testifies, many politicians have cited these petitions as making a crucial difference.[88] Those petitions are, moreover, started by individual citizens. If you believe that there is an issue which is not receiving enough political attention – whether it be the destructive impact of our trade policies, or the power of secretive investment tribunals – consider setting one up yourself.

Perhaps the most important thing you can do is to try to persuade others. The political feasibility of any given reform obviously depends on what other people are likely to do. As we have seen, it may also hinge on how people *expect* their fellow citizens to act. The more we can do to increase the visibility of global justice issues in the political sphere, the better. And the more we can encourage people to think about how they interact with the wider world – and the ways in which this might generate moral duties – the better too. Here, there is room for disagreement about the best strategy. Some scholars have suggested that if we want to motivate people to act to reduce global injustice, we should place greater emphasis on the ways in which we have caused global injustice to arise. If we are somehow *to blame* for particular injustices, then being obliged to recognize that might encourage us to take the problem more seriously.[89] But there is a contrary view. To condemn our fellow citizens for sustaining injustice may actually turn people off from the topic of global justice. Nobody, we might think, wants to feel guilty – and we often manage not to think about things that make us feel that way. If so, positive messages about global justice – which emphasize the remarkable progress the world has made towards ending global poverty, and describe good-news stories about the effectiveness of political or consumer campaigns – may be more effective.[90] In reality, a mixture of the two strategies will probably be necessary. Crucial too may be an element of storytelling. It is all too easy to see the problem of global injustice as a parade of statistics. Artists, authors and film-makers may have an important role to play in bringing home to us the nature of peoples' lives across our planet, and the many connections that link our lives to the lives of outsiders.[91] In this book I have tried to combine a sense of the enormity of the problem of global injustice – and of our role in perpetuating it – with a sense of the real opportunities for change. If I have managed to persuade you of the importance of these issues, then perhaps you can persuade others too.

Notes

Chapter 1: What is the Problem?

1 For a useful guide to extreme poverty, see https:// ourworldindata.org/extreme-poverty

2 For an introduction to the global distribution of wealth, see James Davies, Susanna Sandström, Anthony Shorrocks and Edward N. Wolff (2008) *The Worldwide Distribution of Household Wealth*. UNU-WIDER Discussion Paper 2008/03.

3 See Valentine Moghadam (2005) *The 'Feminization of Poverty' and Women's Human Rights*. Social and Human Sciences Working Paper number 2, UNESCO.

4 The refugees arriving on Europe's shores are of course a small part of a more complex global picture. Many of the world's poorest people are 'internally displaced' – homeless in their country of birth – and very many refugees seek shelter in other very poor countries. For more background on the global

picture, see the United Nation's refugee agency website: http://www.unhcr.org/uk/figures-at-a-glance. html

5 In practice, simple scarcity of water is not the only problem. Sometimes people are simply out-competed by more powerful actors. For instance, poor people's access to clean water is often threatened when multinational corporations come to control water sources. For a discussion of the case of Bolivia, and the ongoing challenge of meeting a basic human right to water, see Madeline Baer (2015) 'From Water Wars to Water Rights: Implementing the Human Right to Water in Bolivia', *Journal of Human Rights* 14.3, 353–76.

6 Tom Burgess et al. (2016) *Water: At What Cost? The State of the World's Water 2016* (Water Aid).

7 Amartya Sen (1999) *Development as Freedom* (Oxford University Press). See also Martha Nussbaum (2011) *Creating Capabilities: The Human Development Approach* (Harvard University Press), and Ingrid Robeyns (2017) *Wellbeing, Freedom and Social Justice: The Capabilities Approach Re-examined* (Open Book Publishers).

8 For more information on the Index, see http://ophi.org.uk/multidimensional-poverty-index/. See also Sabina Alkire and Emma Santos (2010) *Acute Multidimensional Poverty: A New Index for Developing Countries.* United Nations Development Programme Human Development Report Office Background Paper No. 2010/11.

9 World Health Organization (2004) *World Health Report 2004,* available at http://www.who.int/whr/2004/en/

10 Roger Riddell (2011) 'Aiding the World's Poor', in P. Illingworth, T. Pogge and L. Wenar (eds) *Giving Well* (Oxford University Press), p. 87.

11 United Nations (2015) *The World's Women 2015*, chapter 8. For an analysis of the distinctive features of women's disadvantage, see Heather Widdows (2011) *Global Ethics: An Introduction* (Routledge), chapter 11 ('Global Gender Justice').

12 Andrés Castaneda et al. (2016) *Who Are the Poor in the Developing World?* World Bank Policy Research Working Paper 7844.

13 Daron Acemoglu and James Robinson (2012) *Why Nations Fail: The Origins of Power, Prosperity and Poverty* (Profile Books), chapter 9.

14 See https://www.gapminder.org/dollar-street/

15 For an in-depth exploration of the lives of people living in poverty in the UK, see Stephen Armstrong (2017) *The New Poverty* (Verso).

16 For some individual stories of people living on the margins in London, see Alice Bloch and Sonia McKay (2016) *Living on the Margins: Undocumented Migrants in a Global City* (Policy Press).

17 Pedro Olinto et al. (2013) *The State of the Poor*. World Bank Economic Premise No. 125.

18 Paul Collier (2007) *The Bottom Billion* (Oxford University Press).

19 For more information on trends in global poverty, see https://ourworldindata.org/extreme-poverty

20 Richard Easterlin (2000) 'The Worldwide Standard of Living Since 1800', *Journal of Economic Perspectives* 14.1, 7–26.

21 Jan Luiten van Zanden et al. (eds) (2014) *How Was Life? Global Wellbeing Since 1820* (OECD Publishing).

22 Angus Deaton (2013) *The Great Escape* (Princeton University Press).

23 For an overview, see Anthony Pereira (2001) 'Democracies: Emerging or Submerging?', *Dissent* 48, 17–23.

24 For an examination of the US case, see https://www.epi.org/publication/charting-wage-stagnation/

25 For more information, see https://www.economist.com/news/finance-and-economics/21588900-all-around-world-labour-losing-out-capital-labour-pains. See also Francois Bourguignon (2015) *The Globalization of Inequality* (Princeton University Press), chapter 2.

26 World Inequality Lab (2018) *World Inequality Report 2018, Executive Summary*, available at https://wir2018.wid.world/executive-summary.html

27 Thomas Piketty (2013) *Capital in the Twenty-first Century* (Harvard University Press).

28 Branko Milanovic (2016) *Global Inequality* (Harvard University Press), chapter 4.

29 Branko Milanovic (2011) *The Haves and the Have-Nots* (Basic Books), p. 169. For more recent figures on the top 1 per cent, see Sudhir Anand and Paul Segal (2017) 'Who Are the Global Top 1%?', *World Development* 95, 111–26.

30 Anand and Segal, 'Who Are the Global Top 1%?', p. 112.

31 Milanovic, *The Haves and the Have-Nots*, p. 118.

32 Figures courtesy of Paul Segal.

33 Milanovic, *The Haves and the Have-Nots*, p. 113.

34 See the World Bank data at: https://data.worldbank.org/indicator/EN.ATM.CO2E.PC

35 https://data.worldbank.org/indicator/EG.USE.PCAP.KG.OE

36 Arjen Hoekstra and Mesfin Mekonnen (2012) 'The Water Footprint of Humanity', *Proceedings of the National Academy of Sciences* 109.9, 3232–7.
37 For discussion, see Bourguignon, *The Globalization of Inequality*.
38 Milanovic, *Global Inequality*.
39 Jon Messenger and Nikhil Ray (2013) *The Distribution of Hours of Work in Developed and Developing Countries: What Are the Main Differences and Why?* International Labor Organization TRAVAIL Policy Brief 5.
40 Michael Clemens, Claudio Montenegro and Lant Pritchett (2008) *The Place Premium: Wage Differences for Identical Workers Across the US Border.* Center for Global Development Working Paper 148.
41 https://data.unicef.org/data/secondary-education-data/
42 https://blogs.worldbank.org/voices/five-challenges-prevent-financial-access-people-developing-coun tries
43 www.worldbank.org/en/results/2013/04/01/bank ing-on-women-extending-womens-access-to-finan cial-services
44 See, for example, Dani Rodrik (2000) 'Institutions for High-Quality Growth: What They Are and How to Acquire Them', *Studies in Comparative International Development* 35.3, 3–31.
45 For a discussion of 'critical junctures' for institutional reform, see Acemoglu and Robinson (2012) *Why Nations Fail*.
46 For an influential analysis, see Ha-Joon Chang (2002) *Kicking Away the Ladder: Development*

Strategy in Historical Perspective (Anthem Press).

47 See, for instance, Robert Wade (2003) 'What Strategies Are Viable for Developing Countries Today? The World Trade Organization and the Shrinking of "Development Space"', *Review of International Political Economy* 10.4, 621–44.

48 Freedom House (2018) *Freedom in the World Report 2018: Democracy in Decline*, available at https://freedomhouse.org/report/freedom-world/freedom-world-2018

49 For more on the causes and consequences of corruption, see, for instance, Pranab Bardhan (1997) 'Corruption and Development: A Review of Issues', *Journal of Economic Literature* 35.3, 1320–46.

50 Ruth Lister (2004) *Poverty* (Polity). Outsiders must, of course, avoid treating those in poverty as *either* entirely blameworthy for their own fate, *or* entirely heroic. The poor are, like the rest of us, individually heroic at times and blameworthy at others, and usually something in between. For a discussion of the various ways in which the global poor are presented in popular and political discussions, see Diana Tietjens Meyers (2016) *Victims' Stories and the Advancement of Human Rights* (Oxford University Press).

51 Joseph Carens (1992) 'Migration and Morality: A Liberal Egalitarian Perspective', in B. Barry and R. Goodin (eds) *Free Movement* (University of Pennsylvania Press).

52 Julie Rozenberg and Stephane Hallegatte (2018) 'Poor People on the Front Line: The Impacts of Climate Change on Poverty in 2030', in Ravi Kanbur

and Henry Shue (eds) *Climate Justice: Integrating Economics and Philosophy* (Oxford University Press).

53 https://www.reuters.com/article/us-china-coal/in-latest-move-china-halts-over-100-coal-power-projects-idUSKBN151090

54 David Coady, Ian W. H. Parry, Louis Sears and Baoping Shang (2015) *How Large Are Global Energy Subsidies?* International Monetary Fund Working Paper 15/105.

Chapter 2: Why Should You Care?

1 John Rawls (1971) *A Theory of Justice* (Harvard University Press).

2 Karl Marx and Friedrich Engels (2015 [1848]) *The Communist Manifesto* (Penguin Classics); Virginia Woolf (2000 [1938]) 'Three Guineas', in *A Room of One's Own and Three Guineas* (Penguin Classics).

3 Ronald Dworkin (2000) *Sovereign Virtue* (Harvard University Press).

4 See, for instance, Thomas Nagel (2005) 'The Problem of Global Justice', *Philosophy & Public Affairs* 33.2, 113–47, and Michael Blake (2001) 'Distributive Justice, State Coercion, and Autonomy', *Philosophy & Public Affairs* 30.3, 257–96.

5 For a thorough survey and critique of these views, see Arash Abizadeh (2007) 'Cooperation, Pervasive Impact, and Coercion: On the Scope (Not Site) of Distributive Justice', *Philosophy & Public Affairs* 35.4, 318–58.

6 This was, famously, the response of Charles Beitz to John Rawls's assumption that we could largely confine the conversation about justice to the level

of the state. See Beitz (1979) *Political Theory and International Relations* (Princeton University Press).

7 https://www.theguardian.com/environment/2016/ jan/06/more-than-half-of-uks-food-sourced-from-abroad-study-finds

8 For a useful guide from the Office of National Statistics, see https://visual.ons.gov.uk/uk-energy-how-much-what-type-and-where-from/

9 Arjen Hoekstra and Ashok Chapagain (2008) *The Globalization of Water* (Wiley-Blackwell).

10 For an early argument to this effect, see Beitz, *Political Theory and International Relations*. More recently Aaron James has argued that the global economy is a complex system of mutual reliance, and that it needs to treat all of its participants fairly. See James (2012) *Fairness in Practice: A Social Contract for a Global Economy* (Oxford University Press).

11 See Beitz, *Political Theory and International Relations*; Kok-Chor Tan (2005) *Justice Without Borders* (Oxford University Press); and Laura Valentini (2011) *Justice in a Globalized World* (Oxford University Press).

12 Abizadeh suggests that pointing to the 'pervasive impact' we have come to have on one another's lives represents a distinct argument for global justice. See Abizadeh, 'Cooperation, Pervasive Impact, and Coercion'.

13 See, for instance, Simon Caney (2011) 'Humanity, Associations, and Global Justice: In Defence of Humanity-Centred Cosmopolitan Egalitarianism', *The Monist* 94.4, 506–34, and Pablo Gilabert (2012)

From Global Poverty to Global Equality (Oxford University Press).

14 Robert Goodin (1988) 'What Is So Special About our Fellow Countrymen?', *Ethics* 98.4, 663–86.

15 As scholars of global justice have sometimes put it, our place of birth seems to be 'arbitrary' from the moral point of view – something that we do not choose, and which therefore should not have a systematic impact on our life-chances. For more on this idea, see Chris Armstrong (2010) 'National Self-Determination, Global Equality and Moral Arbitrariness', *Journal of Political Philosophy* 18.3, 313–34.

16 See Darrel Moellendorf (2002) *Cosmopolitan Justice* (Westview), and Simon Caney (2005) *Justice Beyond Borders* (Oxford University Press).

17 The two arguments are sometimes called 'relationist' and 'non-relationist'. The first argues that global justice becomes relevant because of changes in the world around us, whereas the second simply points to our shared status as human beings. See Andrea Sangiovanni (2007) 'Global Justice, Reciprocity, and the State', *Philosophy & Public Affairs* 35.1, 3–39.

18 Hanqin Xue (2003) *Transboundary Damage in International Law* (Cambridge University Press).

19 See James Christensen (2017) *Trade Justice* (Oxford University Press).

20 This is true even of philosophers who believe that in general we can give greater weight to the interests of those closest to us. See, for instance, David Miller (2007) *National Responsibility and Global Justice* (Oxford University Press).

21 For useful discussions, see Charles Beitz and Robert Goodin (eds) (2009) *Global Basic Rights* (Oxford University Press), and Henry Shue (1980) *Basic Rights: Famine, Affluence and US Foreign Policy* (Princeton University Press).

22 See Thomas Scanlon (1998) *What We Owe to Each Other* (Harvard University Press), p. 225.

23 Monique Deveaux (2016) 'Beyond the Redistributive Paradigm: What Philosophers Can Learn from Poor-Led Politics', in H. P. Gaisbauer, G. Schweiger and C. Sedmak (eds) *Ethical Issues in Poverty Alleviation* (Springer).

24 Shue, *Basic Rights*.

25 For a discussion of what the very poor might be entitled to do to improve their own position, see Alejandra Mancilla (2016) *The Right of Necessity* (Rowman and Littlefield).

26 Aisha Dodwell, Claire Provost and Cathy Shutt (2017) *Re-Imagining UK Aid*. Global Justice Now.

27 Gilabert, *From Global Poverty to Global Equality*, p. 56.

28 See Chris Armstrong (2012) *Global Distributive Justice: An Introduction* (Cambridge University Press).

29 For useful discussion, see Thomas Pogge (ed.) (2007) *Freedom from Poverty as a Human Right* (Oxford University Press).

30 See, for instance, John Rawls (1999) *The Law of Peoples* (Harvard University Press), and Miller, *National Responsibility and Global Justice*.

31 See Chris Armstrong (2009) 'Global Egalitarianism', *Philosophy Compass* 4.1, 155–71.

32 See Tan, *Justice Without Borders*; Caney, *Justice Beyond Borders*; and Moellendorf, *Cosmopolitan Justice*.

33 For a recent argument to this effect, see Samuel Moyn (2018) *Not Enough: Human Rights in an Unequal World* (Harvard University Press).

34 For an influential account of the core human capacities – or 'capabilities' – which human rights protect, see Martha Nussbaum (2011) *Creating Capabilities: The Human Development Approach* (Harvard University Press).

35 For a discussion of many of these 'instrumental' objections to global inequality, see Charles Beitz (2001) 'Does Global Inequality Matter?', *Metaphilosophy* 32.1–2, 95–112. It is worth noting that even those who deny that global inequalities matter in themselves can sometimes object to them because of their effects. See, for instance, David Miller (2006) 'Collective Responsibility and International Inequality in the Law of Peoples', in R. Martin and D. Reidy (eds) *Rawls's Law of Peoples: A Realistic Utopia?* (Oxford University Press).

36 Lea Ypi (2011) *Global Justice and Avant-Garde Political Agency* (Oxford University Press).

37 William Adams et al. (2004) 'Biodiversity Conservation and the Eradication of Poverty', *Science* 306.5699, 1146–9.

38 Chris Armstrong (2017) *Justice and Natural Resources: An Egalitarian Theory* (Oxford University Press), chapter 10.

39 See, for example, Danny Dorling (2017) *The Equality Effect* (New Internationalist), and Kate Pickett and

Richard Wilkinson (2010) *The Spirit Level: Why Equality is Better for Everyone* (Penguin).

40 Some have argued that we should pay attention to a third factor too. This centres around the question of who *benefits* from global injustices. For more on that idea, see Daniel Butt (2007) 'On Benefiting from Injustice', *Canadian Journal of Philosophy* 37.1, 129–52, and Gerhard Øverland and Bashar Haydar (2014) 'The Normative Implications of Benefiting from Injustice', *Journal of Applied Philosophy* 31.4, 349–62.

41 For a famous early argument to that effect, see Peter Singer (1972) 'Famine, Affluence and Morality', *Philosophy & Public Affairs* 1.3, 229–43. See also Singer (2009) *The Life You Can Save* (Random House).

42 Thomas Pogge has famously emphasized the contribution that the privileged make to sustaining global poverty. See Pogge (2002) *World Poverty and Human Rights* (Polity). For critical responses to his argument, see Alison Jaggar (ed.) (2010) *Thomas Pogge and His Critics* (Polity).

43 For a discussion of these issues, see Iris Young (2006) 'Responsibility and Global Justice: A Social Connection Model', *Social Philosophy and Policy* 23.1, 102–30.

44 For a careful exploration of arguments based on capacity and contribution, see Christian Barry and Gerhard Øverland (2016) *Responding to Global Poverty: Harm, Responsibility and Agency* (Cambridge University Press). See also David Miller (2001) 'Distributing Responsibilities', *Journal of Political Philosophy* 9.4, 453–71.

45 For an influential analysis, see Daron Acemoglu, Simon Johnson and James Robinson (2001) 'The Colonial Origins of Comparative Development: An Empirical Investigation', *American Economic Review* 91.5, 1369–401.

46 For a recent discussion of what we might owe in face of such historical injustices, see Catherine Lu (2017) *Justice and Reconciliation in World Politics* (Cambridge University Press).

47 Kevin Watkins (2002) *Rigged Rules and Double Standards: Trade, Globalisation and the Fight Against Poverty* (Oxfam International).

48 Dev Kar and Joseph Spanjers (2015) *Illicit Financial Flows from Developing Countries, 2003–2012.* Global Financial Integrity, available at http://www. gfintegrity . org / report / illicit - financial - flows - from - developing-countries-2004-2013/

49 https : // www . amnesty . org / en / latest / campaigns / 2017/09/killer-facts-the-scale-of-the-global-arms-trade/

50 Leif Wenar (2016) *Blood Oil* (Oxford University Press).

51 Holly Lawford-Smith (2016) 'Difference-Making and Individuals' Climate-Related Obligations', in C. Heyward and D. Roser (eds) *Climate Justice in a Non-Ideal World* (Oxford University Press).

52 For country-by-country figures, see the World Health Organization's guide at: http://www.who. int/gho/health_workforce/physicians_density/en/

53 For an overview of ethical debates on the issue, see Rebecca Shah (ed.) (2010) *The International Migration of Health Workers: Ethics, Rights and Justice* (Palgrave Macmillan).

54 For a debate on responses to the brain drain, see Gillian Brock and Michael Blake (2015) *Debating Brain Drain* (Oxford University Press).

55 Ayelet Shachar and Ran Hirschl (2014) 'On Citizenship, States, and Markets', *Journal of Political Philosophy* 22.2, 231–57.

56 Reece Jones (2016) *Violent Borders* (Verso).

57 For a good survey of the evidence, see Kieran Oberman (2015) 'Poverty and Immigration Policy', *American Political Science Review* 109.2, 239–51.

58 For a good overview of these debates, see Sarah Fine and Lea Ypi (eds) (2016) *Migration in Political Theory* (Oxford University Press).

59 See, for instance, Andrew Altman and Christopher Heath Wellman (2009) *A Liberal Theory of International Justice* (Oxford University Press).

60 Oberman, 'Poverty and Immigration Policy'.

61 Examples include the *United Nations Declaration on the Right to Development* (1986), and the *Vienna Declaration* (1993).

62 See Robin Attfield (2009) 'Mediated Responsibilities, Global Warming, and the Scope of Ethics', *Journal of Social Philosophy* 40.2, 225–36.

Chapter 3: What Can Be Done?

1 For useful statistics, see http://www.nhsconfed.org/resources/key-statistics-on-the-nhs

2 Anca Gheaus (2013) 'The Feasibility Constraint on the Concept of Justice', *The Philosophical Quarterly* 63.252, 445–64.

3 Pablo Gilabert and Holly Lawford-Smith (2012) 'Political Feasibility: A Conceptual Exploration', *Political Studies* 60.4, 809–25.

4 https://www.oxfam.org.uk/media-centre/press-releases/2018/01/more-than-80-per-cent-of-new-global-wealth-goes-to-top-1-per-cent-while-poorest-half-get-nothing

5 For a discussion of the ideas of Slum Dwellers International, see Monique Deveaux (2016) 'Beyond the Redistributive Paradigm: What Philosophers Can Learn from Poor-Led Politics', in H. P. Gaisbauer, G. Schweiger and C. Sedmak (eds) *Ethical Issues in Poverty Alleviation* (Springer). For more on Via Campesina, see https://viacampesina.org/en/

6 See, for example, Alemayehu Geda and Abebe Shimeles (2007) 'Openness, Trade Liberalization, Inequality and Poverty in Africa', in Jomo K. S. and Jacques Baudot (eds) *Flat World, Big Gaps* (Zed Books).

7 For pioneering discussions of the interrelationships between gender and global justice, see Alison Jaggar (ed.) (2014) *Gender and Global Justice* (Polity).

8 See https://www.un.org/sustainabledevelopment/sustainable-development-goals/. Greater gender equality was also one of the UN's earlier Millennium Development Goals, though its approach was often criticized. See, for instance, Naila Kabeer (2005) 'Gender Equality and Women's Empowerment: A Critical Analysis of the Third Millennium Development Goal', *Gender & Development* 13.1, 13–24.

9 See Anke Graness (2015) 'Is the Debate on "Global Justice" a Global One? Some Considerations in View of Modern Philosophy in Africa', *Journal of Global Ethics* 11.1, 126–40.

10 For some interesting thoughts on what African and Western philosophers might have to learn from one

another, see Katrin Flikschuh (2014) 'The Idea of Philosophical Fieldwork: Global Justice, Moral Ignorance, and Intellectual Attitudes', *Journal of Political Philosophy* 22.1, 1–26. For an example of scholarship on global justice from an African perspective, see Edwin Etieyibo (2017) 'Ubuntu, Cosmopolitanism, and Distribution of Natural Resources', *Philosophical Papers* 46.1, 139–62. See also Mvuselelo Ngcoya (2015) 'Ubuntu: Toward an Emancipatory Cosmopolitanism?', *International Political Sociology* 9.3, 248–62. It is worth remembering, in this context, that Amartya Sen, a scholar who has made a great impact on debates on global justice, is from a developing country (India).

11 Samuel Moyn (2018) *Not Enough: Human Rights in an Unequal World* (Harvard University Press), pp. 113–18.

12 For more detail, see P. N. Agarwala (1983) *The New International Economic Order: An Overview* (Pergamon Press).

13 For a useful discussion, see Joseph Stiglitz (2017) *Globalization and Its Discontents Revisited: Anti-Globalization in the Era of Trump* (Penguin).

14 For some historical background, see Joanne Gowa and Soo Yeon Kim (2005) 'An Exclusive Country Club: The Effects of GATT on Trade, 1950–1994', *World Politics* 57.4, 453–78.

15 Neera Chandhoke (2013) 'Realising Justice', *Third World Quarterly* 34.2, 305–20.

16 Maura O'Connor (2013) 'Subsidizing Starvation', *Foreign Policy*, 13 January, available at https://foreignpolicy.com/2013/01/11/subsidizing-starvation/

17 Joseph Stiglitz (2006) *Making Globalization Work* (Penguin), p. 79.

18 James Christensen (2017) *Trade Justice* (Oxford University Press), chapter 5.

19 Dani Rodrik (1995) 'Getting Interventions Right: How South Korea and Taiwan Grew Rich', *Economic Policy* 10.20, 53–107.

20 For an overview of some of the challenges faced by the WTO, see Uri Dadush (2009) *WTO Reform: The Time to Start Is Now*. Carnegie Endowment for International Peace. Available at https://carnegie endowment.org/files/WTO_reform.pdf

21 House of Commons International Development Committee (2013) *Tax in Developing Countries: Increasing Resources for Development*. See https:// publications.parliament.uk/pa/cm201213/cmselect/ cmintdev/130/130.pdf

22 Dev Kar and Joseph Spanjers (2015) *Illicit Financial Flows from Developing Countries: 2004–2013*. Global Financial Integrity.

23 For a detailed case study, see Martin Hearson and Richard Brooks (2010) *Calling Time: Why SABMiller Should Stop Dodging Taxes in Africa*. ActionAid UK.

24 See Thomas Piketty (2013) *Capital in the Twenty-first Century* (Harvard University Press).

25 Kar and Spanjers, *Illicit Financial Flows*.

26 Peter Dietsch (2015) *Catching Capital: The Ethics of Tax Competition* (Oxford University Press).

27 Gabriel Zucman (2014) 'Taxing across Borders: Tracking Personal Wealth and Corporate Profits', *Journal of Economic Perspectives* 28.4, 121–48.

28 Leif Wenar (2016) *Blood Oil* (Oxford University Press).

29 See, for instance, the work of the Extractive Industries Transparency Initiative (eiti.org).

30 For a pioneering discussion of the potential of Sovereign Wealth Funds, see Angela Cummine (2016) *Citizens' Wealth: Why (and How) Sovereign Funds Should be Managed by the People for the People* (Yale University Press).

31 Stiglitz, *Making Globalization Work*, p. 70. See also Sanjay Reddy (2005) 'Just International Monetary Arrangements', in C. Barry and T. Pogge (eds) *Global Institutions and Responsibilities* (Blackwell).

32 For a good overview of criticisms levelled at the IMF and World Bank, see Meena Krishnamurthy (2015) 'International Financial Institutions', in D. Moellendorf and H. Widdows (eds) *The Routledge Handbook of Global Ethics* (Routledge).

33 See, for instance, Francisco Rodriguez and Dani Rodrik (2000) 'Trade Policy and Economic Growth: A Skeptic's Guide to the Cross-National Evidence'. *NBER Macroeconomics Annual* 15, 261–325.

34 Alemayehu Geda and Abebe Shimeles (2007) 'Openness, Trade Liberalization, Inequality and Poverty in Africa', in Jomo K.S. and Jacques Baudot (eds) *Flat World, Big Gaps* (Zed Books). The former chief economist of the World Bank, François Bourguignon, agrees that these policies contributed to an increase in inequality. See Bourguignon (2015) *The Globalisation of Inequality* (Princeton University Press), p. 110.

35 See, for instance, Rodwan Abouharb and David Cingranelli (2006) 'The Human Rights Effects of

World Bank Structural Adjustment, 1981–2000', *International Studies Quarterly* 50.2, 233–62.

36 Stiglitz, *Making Globalization Work*, p. 142.

37 Dani Rodrik (2008) *One Economics, Many Recipes: Globalization, Institutions, and Economic Growth* (Princeton University Press).

38 For discussion, see Fantu Cheru and Cyril Obi (eds) (2010) *The Rise of China and India in Africa: Challenges, Opportunities and Critical Interventions* (Zed Books).

39 Krishnamurthy, 'International Financial Institutions', p. 236.

40 There is some dispute about exactly what makes a debt 'odious'. For a defence of the idea that a debt is odious when the wider population were not consulted on it, and did not benefit from it, see Seema Jayachandran and Michael Kremer (2006) 'Odious Debt', *American Economic Review* 96.1, 82–92.

41 For an introduction to the issues, see Christian Barry, Barry Herman and Lydia Tomitova (eds) (2007) *Dealing Fairly with Developing Country Debt* (Blackwell).

42 Haley Sweetland Edwards (2016) *Shadow Courts: The Tribunals that Rule Global Trade* (Columbia Global Reports).

43 For a moral critique of the current protection of investors' rights, see Aaron James (2017) 'Investor Rights as Nonsense – On Stilts', in Lisa Herzog (ed.) *Just Financial Markets?* (Oxford University Press).

44 See, most famously, Jeffrey Sachs (2005) *The End of Poverty: How We Can Make it Happen in our Lifetime* (Penguin).

45 See, for instance, Angus Deaton (2013) *The Great Escape* (Princeton University Press), chapter 7.

46 For a careful survey, see Roger Riddell (2008) *Does Foreign Aid Really Work?* (Oxford University Press).

47 Deaton, *The Great Escape*, p. 307.

48 Raj Nallari and Breda Griffith (2011) *Understanding Growth and Poverty: Theory, Policy, and Empirics* (World Bank Publications).

49 Sarah Bermeo (2011) 'Foreign Aid and Regime Change: A Role for Donor Intent', *World Development* 39.11, 2021–31.

50 Paul Collier and David Dollar (2001) 'Can the World Cut Poverty in Half? How Policy Reform and Effective Aid Can Meet International Development Goals', *World Development* 29.11, 1787–802.

51 Jennifer van Heerde-Hudson, David Hudson and Paolo Morini (2018) *Reasons for Giving Aid: A Government Policy in Search of a Public?* DevComms Lab. See: https://devcommslab.org/blog/reasons-for-giving-aid-a-government-policy-in-search-of-a-public/

52 In perhaps the most scathing critique of the aid industry, the author is clear that her critique of aid is focused on the government-to-government type. See Dambisa Moyo (2010) *Dead Aid: Why Aid is not Working and How there is another Way for Africa* (Penguin).

53 The idea of rigorously assessing the effectiveness of aid is often associated with the 'effective altruism' movement. For more on that movement, see William MacAskill (2015) *Doing Good Better: How Effective Altruism Can Help You Make a Difference* (Gotham).

54 www.givedirectly.org

55 For recent assessments, see https://www.givewell. org/charities/give-directly. See also Jessica Hagen-Zanker et al. (2016) *Cash Transfers: What Does the Evidence Say?* (Overseas Development Institute).

56 Martin Ravallion (2014) 'On the Role of Aid in *The Great Escape*', *The Review of Income and Wealth* 60.4, 967–84.

57 See, for instance, Lant Pritchett (2006) *Let Their People Come: Breaking the Gridlock on International Labor Mobility* (Center for Global Development).

58 Michael Clemens (2011) 'Economics and Emigration: Trillion-Dollar Bills on the Sidewalk?', *Journal of Economic Perspectives* 25.3, 83–106.

59 Kieran Oberman (2015) 'Poverty and Immigration Policy', *American Political Science Review* 109.2, 239–51.

60 Yéro Baldé (2011) 'The Impact of Remittances and Foreign Aid on Savings/Investment in Sub-Saharan Africa', *African Development Review* 23.2, 247–62. See also Adams Bodomo (2013) 'African Diaspora Remittances are Better than Foreign Aid Funds: Diaspora-Driven Development in the 21st Century', *World Economics* 14.4, 21–9.

61 Jean-Louis Combes, Christian Hubert Ebeke, Sabine Mireille, Ntsama Etoundi and Thierry Urbain Yogo (2014) 'Are Remittances and Foreign Aid a Hedge Against Food Price Shocks in Developing Countries?', *World Development* 54, 81–98.

62 Pritchett, *Let Their People Come*, pp. 74–5.

63 Branko Milanovic (2016) *Global Inequality* (Harvard University Press), pp. 151–4. See also

Martin Ruhs (2013) *The Price of Rights: Regulating International Labor Migration* (Princeton University Press).

64 A searchable database of arms manufacturers is maintained by the Stockholm International Peace Research Institute. See https://www.sipri.org/databases/armsindustry

65 Daniel Mohanty and Annie Shiel (2018) *With Great Power: Modifying US Arms Sales to Reduce Civilian Harm*. Center for Civilians in Conflict.

66 Rachel Stohl and Suzette Grillot (2009) *The International Arms Trade* (Polity), chapter 2.

67 James Christensen (2018) 'Arming the Outlaws: On the Moral Limits of the Arms Trade', *Political Studies*, https://doi.org/10.1177/0032321718754516.

68 Mohanty and Shiel, *With Great Power*.

69 For an argument to that effect, see *Goals Not Guns: How the Sustainable Development Goals and the Arms Trade Treaty Are Interlinked*, Arms Treaty Monitor and Oxfam, 2017.

70 For more information, see https://www.greenclimate.fund/home

71 Chris Armstrong (2017) *Justice and Natural Resources: An Egalitarian Theory* (Oxford University Press), chapter 10.

72 Chris Armstrong (2015) 'Fairness, Free-riding, and Rainforest Protection', *Political Theory* 44.1, 106–30.

73 For more information, see: https://www.undp.org/content/sdfinance/en/home/solutions/debt-for-nature-swaps.html. For some concerns about these proposals, see Nicole Hassoun (2012) 'The Problem of Debt-for-Nature Swaps from a Human Rights

Perspective', *Journal of Applied Philosophy* 29.4, 359–77.

74 For a fairly enthusiastic account of the potential of the Fair Trade movement, see Daniel Jaffee (2007) *Brewing Justice: Fair Trade Coffee, Sustainability, and Survival* (University of California Press). For a discussion of its potential limitations, see April Linton, Cindy Chiayuan Liou and Kelly Ann Sha (2004) 'A Taste of Trade Justice: Marketing Global Social Responsibility Via Fair Trade Coffee', *Globalizations* 1.2, 223–46. For a discussion which assesses Fair Trade from the point of view of global justice, see Nicole Hassoun (2018) 'Fair Trade Under Fire: How to Think about Fair Trade in Theory and Practice', in C. Brown and R. Eckersley (eds) *The Oxford Handbook of International Political Theory* (Oxford University Press).

75 Valentin Beck (2018) 'Consumer Boycotts as Instruments for Structural Change', *Journal of Applied Philosophy*, https://doi.org/10.1111/japp.12301

76 Beck, 'Consumer Boycotts'.

77 For a generally positive overview, see Franziska Bieri (2016) *From Blood Diamonds to the Kimberley Process: How NGOs Cleaned up the Global Diamond Industry* (Routledge).

78 See the report entitled *Wasted Capital and Stranded Assets* (The Carbon Tracker Initiative, 2013), available at https://www.carbontracker.org/reports/unburnable-carbon-wasted-capital-and-stranded-assets/

79 William MacAskill (2015) 'Does Divestment Work?' *The New Yorker*, 20 October.

80 The charity Giving What We Can recommends 10 per cent. See https://www.givingwhatwecan.org/. The philosopher Peter Singer, meanwhile, has argued for a 5 per cent commitment. See Peter Singer (2009) *The Life You Can Save* (Random House).

81 https://www.givingwhatwecan.org/get-involved/myths-about-aid/

82 Effectiveness is just one of many worries that ordinary citizens raise about aid. For responses to this and other worries, see Singer, *The Life You Can Save*, chapter 3.

83 www.givewell.org

84 https://www.charitynavigator.org/

85 See also MacAskill, *Doing Good Better*.

86 https://www.givewell.org/charities/give-directly

87 Henry Shue (1988) 'Mediating Duties', *Ethics* 98.4, 687–704.

88 https://secure.avaaz.org/page/en/highlights/

89 See Holly Lawford-Smith (2012) 'The Motivation Question: Arguments from Justice and from Humanity', *British Journal of Political Science* 42.3, 661–78. See also Andrew Dobson (2006) 'Thick Cosmopolitanism', *Political Studies* 54.1, 165–84.

90 John David Cameron (2018) 'Communicating Cosmopolitanism and Motivating Global Citizenship', *Political Studies* 66.3, 718–34. There is a difficult line to tread here. At the same time as emphasizing the good that people in the West can potentially do, it is important to avoid a 'saviour' mentality, or to downplay our own role in perpetuating injustices. See Serene Khader (1998) 'Victims' Stories and the Postcolonial Politics of Empathy', *Metaphilosophy* 49.1–2, 13–26.

91 Martha Nussbaum (1994) 'Patriotism and Cosmopolitanism', *Boston Review*, 1 October. See also Judith Lichtenberg (2014) *Distant Strangers: Ethics, Psychology, and Global Poverty* (Cambridge University Press), p. 2.

Index

Index